2/6

K/S

KH/
230R

THE ARTISTS' MANUAL OF PIGMENTS.

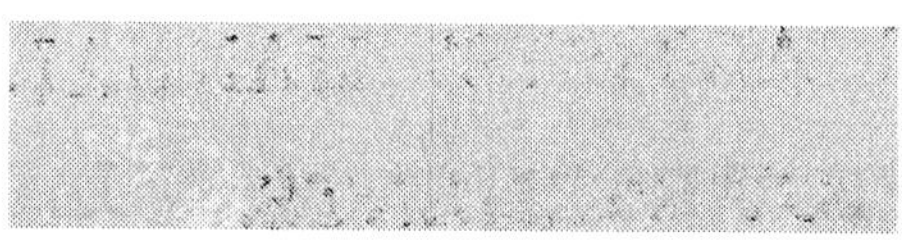

THE

ARTISTS' MANUAL

OF

PIGMENTS

SHOWING

THEIR COMPOSITION, CONDITIONS OF PERMANENCY, NON-PERMANENCY, AND ADULTERATIONS; EFFECTS IN COMBINATION WITH EACH OTHER AND WITH VEHICLES; AND THE MOST RELIABLE TESTS OF PURITY

TOGETHER WITH

The Science and Art Department's Examination Questions on Painting

BY

H. C. STANDAGE

AUTHOR OF "CEMENTS, PASTES, GLUES, AND GUMS," "WATER-COLOUR PIGMENTS," "USE AND ABUSE OF COLOURS AND MEDIUMS IN OIL-PAINTING," ETC. ETC.

Third Edition, Revised

LONDON

CROSBY LOCKWOOD AND SON

7, STATIONERS' HALL COURT, LUDGATE HILL

1896

LONDON:
PRINTED BY J. S. VIRTUE AND CO., LIMITED,
CITY ROAD.

PREFACE.

Of late years the question of the deterioration in hue of modern English pictures is one that has occupied an important position in art circles. These pictures are found to be unpossessed of that permanency of colouring so noticeable in the works of old masters of foreign schools. The "why and the wherefore" for these changes are not far to seek; they may be attributed to the ignorance of the modern artist as regards the actual nature of the materials he employs. This ignorance is due to his being practically unacquainted with the chemical nature and qualities of his pigments and vehicles, whereas "old masters" were their own chemists; and notwithstanding that chemical knowledge in their time was of the most elementary kind, they perforce, through making their own pigments, were compelled to become possessed of some knowledge regarding the chemical reactions occurring between mixtures of pigments with each other and with vehicles. This knowledge was sufficient to enable them to avoid dangerous immixtures of pigments and vehicles; but undoubtedly the great success of the permanence of their colouring was due to the use of an oleo-resinous medium instead of pure oil, or oil and spirits, as now used.

Another cause of the non-permanence of modern paintings is to be found in the use of impure pigments. The manufacture of pigments has become a trade, and, like many others, it is one not free from the vicious practice of selling a sophisticated article when a pure one is not absolutely insisted on by the purchaser. Pure pigments can be bought, but while there is a demand for cheap paints, and the artist is careless enough not to satisfy himself that what he buys is perfectly pure, the supply of adulterated pigments will be kept up. This supply is greatly encouraged by the huge host of amateur painters and manufacturers of "pot-boilers," who have no name to lose by bad workmanship, and who, moreover, are not wealthy enough to afford the price demanded for pure materials.

Still another cause of the decadence of colouring in modern paintings is to be traced in the desire, on the part of well-known artists, to obtain startling, brilliant, or surprising effects of colouring, the means by which this desire is gratified being carelessly ignored so that they gain their wishes. These painters recklessly make the most pernicious immixtures of pigments. The results show themselves a few years subsequently, and the picture is worse than a bad imitation of itself in its former state.

But whatever the cause, the fact remains; modern pictures are far from permanent. This is saying very little for art and its patrons, for the knowledge of the means of painting good sound work is not difficult to obtain, although through indolence, prejudice, or self-conceited satisfaction in their own individual method of working, modern artists do not trouble themselves to obtain it.

Many pigments are known under several names. An artist may buy a colour under one name, and never dream of its being identical in composition and qualities with one of another name. In the chapters on individual pigments I have given the general equivalents by which a pigment is commonly known. The reader will, therefore, be able to identify a pigment bearing half-a-dozen names. The paragraphs on the "Chemical Names and

Composition" give the chemical nature and qualities of each pigment in its perfect form. This is necessary, because artists are not chemists, and elaborate explanations on this point would be of little value to them.

The paragraphs on the "Artistic Qualities" will, I hope, prove of exceptional value. Those on the "Permanency and Non-Permanency" of pigments are based on a knowledge of the chemical and physical reactions that occur, or are likely to occur, between mixtures of pigments.

The information on "General Adulterations" is given that artists may know what to expect, and the "Tests for Purity" have been so selected as to allow of their being practically worked out by persons devoid of chemical knowledge. Artists' colourmen may not be to blame for supplying a sophisticated article if they find a demand for it, but artists of repute *are* to blame if they do not take every means in their power to ascertain that the colour they use is in its purest form.

The matter contained in Chapters I. to VI. was first published by the Author under the title of "The Artists' Table of Pigments," a work now out of print. But the whole of the remainder of the present volume is now published for the first time.

Chapter VII., on "Chemical Reactions occurring between Pigments, &c.," will, I think, demonstrate that although painting is an art, its foundation rests on scientific principles if the work is to be of a sound character.

Chapter VIII. sets before the reader so much of colour science as can be serviceable to a non-scientific person; while Chapters IX., X., XI. are intended for students and those amateurs who wish to acquire a knowledge of the technical processes involved in painting. The Science and Art Department Examination Questions on Painting form Chapter XII.

The following pigments have been included in those chapters in which their hues seem to entitle them to be classed:—New Blue, Permanent Blue, Mars Orange, Mars Yellow, Orient Yellow, Mineral Yellow, Mars Red, Purple Lake, Mars Brown, Mineral Gray, Neutral Tint, Payne's Gray, Rubens Madder.

H. C. S.

31, DELVINO ROAD, FULHAM, S.W.
November, 1885.

NOTE TO THE THIRD EDITION.

THE fact that a Third Edition of the "ARTISTS' MANUAL OF PIGMENTS" is called for, is sufficient proof that the work fulfils its purpose of being a helping guide to the Fine Art Painter in the use of Pigments. This point is emphasized by the fact that since the publication of the last edition other books on Pigments have been issued, of which the Author feels justified in saying that, whatever their merits in point of accuracy of information or otherwise, the information is not so given as to be sufficiently easy of assimilation in practice, so that they fail to meet the wants of the painter. Hence the continued demand for the present manual.

The Author takes the present opportunity of warning artists against the use of petroleum and paraffin, as advocated by a French writer. These articles do not possess the permanency claimed for them by M. Vibert, and are (in the Author's judgment) practically valueless as media for colours in the fine arts.

With the exception of the correction of a few typographical errors the contents of this little book remain as in the last edition.

SUNNYSIDE,
ERDINGTON, WARWICKSHIRE.
July, 1896.

CONTENTS.

CONTENTS.

CHAPTER VI.

BROWN AND BLACK PIGMENTS.

CHAPTER VII.

CHEMICAL REACTIONS OCCURRING BETWEEN TWO OR MORE PIGMENTS, BETWEEN PIGMENT AND VEHICLE, ETC.

CHAPTER VIII.

COLOUR NAMES AND DEFINITIONS.

THE

ARTISTS' MANUAL OF PIGMENTS.

CHAPTER I.

WHITE PIGMENTS.

BARYTA WHITE (also known as Constant or Permanent White).

Chemical Names and Composition.—This white is a sulphate of barium, or "baric sulphate" of the chemist, and known as "heavy spar" by the mineralogist. In composition it consists of 137 atoms of barium, 32 atoms of sulphur, and 64 atoms of oxygen. The constituents in the above proportions constitute the *neutral* sulphate of barium. Constant white is occasionally a mixture of carbonate and sulphate of barium.

Note.—When carelessly made this white is not entirely freed from sulphuric acid. Such acid is injurious to its stability.

Artistic Qualities.—This white is of a beautiful though

bluish-tinted white, dense in tone, but deficient in body. It has a darker tone when moist (*i.e.* when being used) than it has when dry. Gum-water destroys or mars the whiteness. It is of good use for fresco, silicious, and water-colour painting.

Conditions of Permanency.—This white is perfectly permanent under all conditions. Sulphuretted hydrogen gas does not affect its colour, nor does any pigment containing sulphur, since the sulphide of barium which might be formed is also white. This is a great desideratum where purity of high lights is requisite, or a white has to be used almost pure. Strong light, darkness, oxygen, lead, or iron, have no injurious action on the purity of this white.

Conditions of Non-Permanency.—The neutral sulphate is the one the artist should employ, because the acid sulphate is semi-stable, since the free acid is apt to be injurious when brought into contact with pigments affected by acids, or on some of the oils and other vehicles used. In some cases an acid will darken a colour; in others it bleaches or robs a pigment of its colour, and in all cases, other whites as well, it has a disintegrating action.

General Adulterations.—Lead salts (usually carbonates) are sometimes added to this white to give it body, *i.e.* covering power. Zinc salts (usually the oxide) are also added to give it whiteness.

Tests for Purity and Nature of Adulterants.—If the white be pure, no reaction will be shown by adding a little solution of sulphuretted hydrogen to the pigment. If a lead salt be present, this test agent will cause a black precipitate to be formed. To test for the presence of other metals, use the tests given under white lead. To detect free sulphuric acid, add a slip of blue litmus paper to a washing of the pigment; if the blue colour is turned red, free acid is present. If the white paint is found to contain much free acid, it may be greatly divested of the acid by washing the pigment with distilled water. This may be done by placing the pigment on a filter-paper, and directing a stream of water on to it from the wash-bottle. In this operation the filter paper containing the pigment is supported in a glass funnel.

Remarks.—The amorphous state of the sulphate is the best for use on the palette, because in this state its covering power is best. This white is the best to use with sulphides of metals, lead or iron pigments, *e.g.* cadmium yellow, vermilion, yellow and orange chromes (of lead), Indian, Venetian, and other reds, of which the basis is iron, and red and yellow ochres. The neutral sulphate should be tested for free sulphuric acid, since if present the permanency of the white itself is weakened, and this acid has also power to destroy other pigments.

BLANC D'ARGENT (or Silver White, or French White).

Chemical Names and Composition.—This white is a white obtained from lead by a process different to that employed in making flake white.

Artistic Qualities.—This white has less body than flake white, but is of exquisite whiteness.

Conditions of Permanency.—This white is just as stable, no more, no less, than white lead used in a similar manner.

Conditions of Non-Permanency.—It suffers, in company with white lead, since this white possesses all the deleterious characteristics of the more frequently used white lead.

General Adulterations.—Chalk and baric sulphate are those most chiefly to be searched for.

Tests for Purity and Nature of Adulterants.—The tests given under "White Lead" apply to this pigment.

Remarks.—This white is sometimes preferred by artists as a white probably owing to its fanciful name, but it should be vigorously excluded from use, like the rest of the whites made from lead.

FLAKE WHITE (when levigated called Body White).

Chemical Names and Composition.—Oxidised carbonate of lead, or a compound of protocarbonate and hydrated oxide of lead.

Artistic Qualities.—Identical under every circumstance with white lead or other lead carbonates. This white has the best body of all white leads.

Conditions of Permanency.—The permanency of this white varies according to the mode of preparation.

Conditions of Non-Permanency.—Refer to white lead for these conditions.

General Adulterations.—This white is sometimes not entirely freed from the acid engendered in its manufacture.

Tests for Purity and Nature of Adulterants.—Refer to the tests given under the heading of white lead.

Remarks.—This white is called by the artists' colourmen "common white." It owes its flaky character to the mode of preparation, and takes its name from the scrolls or plates in which it is formed. If it contains free acid, it is still more injurious to other pigments than when pure, as will be seen on referring to the general remarks at the end of this chapter on normal, basic, and acid carbonates of lead. This white is occasionally equal to Chinese white in colour, and generally superior in body to all other white leads. The presence of the hydrate of lead decreases the opacity of the product, according to the greater proportion in which it is present.

WHITE LEAD (known also as Ceruse, Cremnitz, Dutch, Flemish, Hamburg, Venetian, or Roman White).

Chemical Names and Composition.—The whites known under the above names are all carbonates of lead. Cremnitz white is usually pure white lead. Dutch white contains 24 per cent. of white lead and 75 per cent. of baric sulphate. If they contain hydrate of lead the components of water are present. Hamburg white is a mixture of two parts heavy spar (baric sulphate), and the remainder white lead. Venetian white is sulphate of barium (basic sulphate) and carbonate of lead in equal parts.

Artistic Qualities.—These lead whites possess good body. The "body" (by which is meant covering power) is better in proportion as the carbonate is whiter and heavier. These and all lead whites are easy to work, are very opaque, and impart their quality to pigments compounded with it. Cremnitz white is the whitest of white leads. When mixed with barytes white, white lead is semi-transparent. Strong light, especially sunlight, will sometimes restore the brightness of tarnished white lead; so also will hydroxyl, *i.e.* peroxide of hydrogen, or *water*, plus a second atom of oxygen.

Conditions of Permanency.—Linton says white leads compound without injury with ultramarine, red and orange leads, yellow and orange chromes, yellow, orange, and red cadmiums, aureolin, the ochres, and Indian red, viridian, and also oxides of chromium. We criticise this assertion elsewhere.

Conditions of Non-Permanency.—Much oil or varnish destroys these whites, partly by abstracting oxygen in their process of "drying," and partly by becoming brown themselves. Also, sulphides of metals and sulphuretted hydrogen (the symbol for this compound is SH_2, which will be used in future) darken this white. White lead destroys the tints formed by it with lakes (madder lakes excepted), probably by oxygenating them, and so bleaching their colour. These whites are injured by darkness and impure air, and blacken sooner in oil (due possibly to the loss of oxygen) than in water. They are unsafe to use in fresco and distemper painting, and in crayon. They are all very fugitive, and lose their opacity, allowing whatever paint is beneath to show through them. Massicot, red and orange leads, orpiment or king's yellow, and patent yellow, are injured by white lead. Hydrated oxide of lead gives white lead less covering power, and it turns to a brownish hue.

General Adulterations.—These are whitening, sulphate of barium, sulphate of lime (*i.e.* gypsum or "plaster of Paris"), oxide of lead, and carbonate of lime. These substances are inimical to the perfect drying of white lead, and lessen its body and brightness, and darken the oil vehicles.

Tests for Purity and Nature of Adulterants.—If pure, white lead is entirely dissolved by nitrous or acetic acid, either of which leaves a clear liquid. Distinguished from other white pigments, when acted on by SH_2 or a sulphide by the formation of a black sulphide of lead. To test for whitening, add dilute nitrous acid, boil in a test-tube, and then add hydrochloric acid; filter the liquid, and to the filtered solution add ammonic oxalate. A white deposit indicates whitening. To test for a barium salt, employ the blowpipe test, inner flame. A green coloration of the flame indicates barium; with the same test, a red coloration indicates calcium or gypsum, *i.e.* sulphate of lime.

Remarks.—The cause why white lead works so easily under the brush is owing to its saponifying with the oil (*i.e.* entering into a chemical union therewith), whence it becomes linoleate of lead, or "lead soap." This chemical union causes the pellicles of oil to be almost destroyed as a protective coating, since the new body thus formed is easily acted on by influences that would not attack the oil if the latter formed simply a coat or covering to the pigment, as it should do. Besides this union, white lead also parts with some of its oxygen to the oil, whereby the latter becomes dry and hard, thus leaving the metallic lead more open to the action of sulphurous fumes, or to pigments possessing sulphur, to be turned into the black sulphide of lead. Cremnitz white is also known as Vienna white, being brought from Vienna in cakes of a cubical form. It is the brightest white that is used in oil, but possesses rather less body than flake white, because the particles are finer.

Roman white is of the purest colour, and differs only from Blanc d'Argent in the warm flesh tints of its surface when in large masses.

ZINC WHITE, or Chinese White.

Chemical Names and Composition.—Oxide of zinc, or zincic oxide. This white consists either of 65 atoms of zinc to 16 of oxygen, or else it is the anhydrous oxide, the hydrate oxide, or hydrated basic carbonate of zinc.

Artistic Qualities.—This white wants body in oil, but it is the best possible white in water-colour. It is a bad dryer, although it is an excellent "dryer" itself for oils. Zinc white may be mixed with various pigments possessing durability, such as the oxides of iron, charcoal, oxides of manganese, ultramarine, &c., and will then furnish colours the tones of which will remain permanent; and this is a great advantage in painting, whether alone or mixed with other pigments. Zinc white is used for oil and water-colours, and for varnish and distemper painting.

Conditions of Permanency.—This white is thoroughly permanent under all conditions of use or mixture. It does not form a soap with oils and fats. It retains its opacity, and is not fugacious, like white lead. It is most durable in silicious painting or stereochromy, in which process of painting it forms chemical compounds with potash and silicon, which are stable.

Conditions of Non-Permanency.—It is not impermanent under any circumstances.

General Adulterations.—These are carbonate of lead and

sometimes carbonate of lime, and kaolin (*i.e.* china clay), and starch.

Tests for Purity and Nature of Adulterants.—If the zinc white be pure, it is perfectly soluble in sulphuric acid, and does not effervesce during solution like white lead. To detect lead, add SH_2, and if salts of lead be present, a black precipitate is formed; the borax bead, with the blowpipe test, will be purple if manganese be added. If iron is added, that metal will be obtained in a metallic powder when the pigment is heated on charcoal with carbonate of soda under the blowpipe analysis.

Remarks.—This is a good pigment when well prepared. Since it does not saponify with oils, this white is the safest to use where permanency of opacity is required. Although in itself it is less opaque, it possesses less body than white lead. It may, however, be laid over white lead when that has dried, to preserve the latter from subsequent deleterious influences, and this permanency and opacity of the whites will be maintained. Chinese white replaces the ordinary zinc white in water colours.

Normal, Basic, and Acid Carbonates.

The metal that yields the largest number of whites is *lead*, and the best white obtained from it, suitable for the artist, is the *carbonate.*

Now, carbonates are usually divided into *normal*, *basic*, and *acid.*

The *normal* carbonate is one in which the equivalent of the metal is united with the compound represented by the formula CO_3.

A *basic* carbonate contains water; that is, the hydrogen in the water that has united with the carbonate acts similarly to a *base*, or the opposite action to that of an acid; while an *acid* carbonate is one that has not been entirely freed from an acid radicle.

Most carbonates are easily decomposed by heat. The carbonates of the heavy metals are all decomposed at a low red heat, giving off carbonic anhydride (CO_2) and leaving a residue of metal or of oxide.

The carbonates of the fixed alkali metals are not decomposed by the strongest heat. At a very high temperature they are somewhat neutralised. The acid carbonates of the alkalies are reduced by heat to normal carbonates, with evolution of CO_2.

It may be wondered why we go so deeply into chemical points, but here it is that a knowledge of these points is valuable. Thus, alkalies decompose or destroy the materials used as vehicles in painting; therefore, if a basic—*i.e.* an alkaline—carbonate be employed, we can see that it will commence a chemical action on the oil or vehicle with which it is incorporated, and this action may be such as to prove injurious to the picture; whilst, again, an acid carbonate may be accidentally incorporated with a pigment—perhaps the oxide of a metal, and, since an oxide is a *base*, and tends to neutralise an acid, here again chemical action would be set up, the result of which could not but be damaging, even to the neutralising or fading of the tint.

The greater number of fixed oils by exposure to the air become viscid and rancid, in which state they contain free acid. Now we have seen that bases and oxides neutralise acids, therefore, a basic carbonate, or an oxide, by acting on the "free acid" would again set up chemical action and so prove injurious.

Therefore the only carbonate fit for the purpose of a pigment is the normal or neutral one, and hence the value of having a means of testing the nature of the pigment, or, in other words, its purity.

Instructions in Blowpipe Testing.—In many cases where it is desired to know which metal the pigment is a salt of, the blowpipe gives a readier means than what is known as the "wet process" of analysis, therefore the method of using this handy utensil should be thoroughly understood by the operator, especially so since the operation is so simple.

In the first place, a steady flame is requisite. This is to be obtained thus: Close the lips and puff out the cheeks with air drawn through the nostrils; while the cheeks are so inflated, press the blowpipe between the lips, and by the muscles of the cheeks force the air through the pipe, the supply being kept constant by drawing it in through the nostrils.

This action will require some little practice to acquire, but it will be soon and easily learnt after a few trials.

Having managed to acquire a constant blast, direct the nozzle of the pipe on to the flame of a spirit-lamp so that the flame is a horizontal one. This flame will then become pointed, and possess two distinct points; *e.g.* in the interior of the flame is a *blue* coloured cone, while the outer portion is of a *reddish* tinge; this blue point is termed the *reducing* flame, because it reduces metals from their oxides; whilst the outer cone or shell is termed the *oxidising* flame, since this oxidises salts. The blue flame consists of particles of unburnt carbon, particles with which oxygen has not combined, and therefore combustion has not taken place, whilst the outer flame owes its intense heat and incandescence to the violent union taking place between the oxygen of the air and the carbon particles of the spirit.

To utilise this blowpipe flame, select a piece of charcoal free from knots and of fine texture and close grain, trim it up somewhat prism-shaped, and scoop out a hollow cavity at one end, into which put the salt to be tested, gradually bringing the other end of the charcoal in the flame and then cautiously raise this end; the flame shooting lengthwise of the charcoal; the experiment will direct wherever the oxidising or reducing flame is to be employed. If the oxidising flame, the point only is employed, and this must not be directed on to the salt at once, or the whole would be scattered about, but gradually brought into it as described; at the same time the full source of the blast must not be attained until the flux begins to fuse.

Another method of employing the blowpipe flame, instead of the charcoal method, is to make use of a platinum wire and borax bead. Thus, take a piece of narrow soft glass tube, six inches long, heat it in the middle in the spirit flame, and when beginning to bend pull the ends apart and snap the tube in the centre; take one of these pieces, and through the narrow end thus formed insert a piece of platinum wire four inches long, about three inches remaining out of the tube. By directing the blowpipe on to this narrow portion the wire will be firmly fused in the glass, the latter thus forming a handle that will prevent the heat reaching the fingers. The end of the wire should be formed into a loop about three-sixteenths of an inch in diameter. To employ this instrument, dip the loop into a little hydrochloric acid to free the wire from corrosion. Never dip anything into the bottle of acid, for that might render the whole impure, but keep a little acid in a small test-tube or watch-glass. When testing by means of a platinum wire, hold it in the lamp or blowpipe flame, dip into a little borax, hold in the lamp again until the borax is fused into a clear glass bead; then, moistening this bead in acid again, dip into the salt to be tested, and fuse in the inner or outer flame as the instructions direct.

To free the wire from this bead, open the loop with the thumb and finger, free from corrosion with the finger nail, and purify by dipping in acid and heating in flame, after which it is fit for next test.

CHAPTER II.

GREEN PIGMENTS.

CHROME GREENS.

Chemical Names and Composition.—Oxides of chromium or hydrated or anhydrous chromic oxide. Sesquioxide of chromium. Consists of oxygen and chromium combined either by wet or dry chemical processes; it is pale or deep, bright or subdued, opaque or transparent in appearance.

Artistic Qualities.—These oxides when used in water require much gum; when in oil, in which they dry well, they afford pure, natural, and durable tints.

Conditions of Permanency.—When anhydrous they can be used in enamelling, and are all thoroughly permanent, neither injuring nor being injured by other pigments, nor by foul gas, air, damp, nor light.

Conditions of Non-Permanency.—When hydrated they cannot be used in enamelling. Mixtures of chrome yellows with Prussian and other blues are less permanent than the actual pigments.

General Adulterations.—Chrome yellow, Prussian or other blues.

Tests for Purity and Nature of Adulterants.—Test for presence of yellows made from lead or baryta or Prussian blue made from iron in usual way. If pure these tests will give no result. If the tests affect the pigment, we may know that it is not a true chrome green.

Remarks.—It is better to use the actual pigment than a green compounded on the palette. Mixed with raw sienna, gives a sombre and semi-transparent green.

NATIVE GREEN (Pure Chrome Green, Green Oxide of Chromium, Opaque Oxide of Chromium, or Chrome Oxide).

Chemical Names and Composition.—Is an impure native chrome ochre, prepared artificially for the palette. When obtained anhydrous by dry methods from the metal chromium, it is the only chrome oxide available in enamelling.

Artistic Qualities.—Is a cold, sober, sage green, deep-toned, opaque, and dull; very dense and powerful. In flat tints the oxide does not wash well in water.

Conditions of Permanency.—Unchangeable in themselves and do not affect colours mixed with them.

Conditions of Non-Permanency.—Chrome greens containing Prussian blue are acted upon by alkalies, and those containing lead suffer the disadvantages incidental to lead pigments.

General Adulterations.—Artificially prepared, chrome greens are often made by mixing solutions of lead and iron with prussiate and chromate of potash or by adding potassic chromate and then plumbic acetate to a solution of Prussian blue in oxalic acid, whence lead or iron may be accidentally present as adulterants.

Tests for Purity and Nature of Adulterants.—Pure chromium greens when subjected to great heat retain their colour unchanged.

Remarks.—Should be used with a delicate hand to prevent heaviness. In tints with white it is delicate and pleasing, being silvery and luminous; good for atmospheric effects.

TRANSPARENT OXIDE OF CHROMIUM.

Chemical Names and Composition.—A compound of oxygen and chromium.

Artistic Qualities.—Is deficient in body, and only useful in oils. Is a pale greyish green in powder.

Conditions of Permanency.—Unchangeable and harmless to other compounding pigments.

Remarks.—A yellowish green of some depth, moderately bright, in oil not very pure or clear.

EMERALD GREEN (Schweinfurt, Vienna, Imperial, Brunswick, and Mitis Green).

Chemical Names and Composition.—It is a cupric aceto-arsenite.

Artistic Qualities.—These greens, which are identical in body but variously named, are lighter, more opaque and vivid than Scheele's green. Reflect light well; dry badly in oil, but better in water. Compounded with aureolin they are softened and semi-transparent.

Conditions of Permanency.—Are perhaps the most permanent of the copper greens, both alone and in tint with white. Are not much affected by damp or foul air..

Conditions of Non-Permanency.—Cannot be used in fresco or silicious painting. Cadmic sulphide also would decompose them with formation of the brown sulphide of copper.

General Adulterations.—Brunswick green is often but a mixture of chromate of lead and Prussian blue.

Remarks.—Should be used only in small quantities, or its brightness toned down by introduction of masses of other greens. Contains arsenic, so should be used with caution.

MALACHITE (Mountain, or Hungary Green).

Chemical Names and Composition.—Is a hydrated dicarbonate of copper, combined with a white earth. Formed native by the constant dropping of water saturated with carbonic acid, and holding in solution the oxide of copper.

Artistic Qualities.—For artistic purposes it is prepared artificially; the latter is not so bright as the native variety, which gives greens varying from emerald to grass green, inclining to grey.

Conditions of Permanency.—Durable in pure air and light.

Conditions of Non-Permanency.—Blackened by bad air and age, and exclusion from light. Converted into blues by the action of alkalies. Inferior in durability to Scheele's greens.

General Adulterations.—The general adulterants of these three greens consist of various mixtures of blues and yellows.

Remarks.—Scarcely fit for the artists' palette.

SAP GREEN (Verde Vessie, Iris or Bladder Green).

Chemical Names and Composition.—Is the inspissated juice of buckthorn berries, or made from the green leaves of the woad, or the blue flowers of the iris, &c.

Artistic Qualities.—Is dark in colour, of a fine natural yellowish transparent green. Useful in water for flower painting.

Conditions of Permanency.—Fairly durable in water colours, less so in oil.

Conditions of Non-Permanency.—Imperfect as a pigment, as it attracts moisture, and is thus liable to engender mildew. Fugitive in course of time.

General Adulterations.—Adulterated with other vegetable green colours, such as extract of coffee-berries.

Tests for Purity and Nature of Adulterants.—When pure has a glossy fracture.

Remarks.—Similar pigments obtained from coffee-berries, and named Venetian and emerald greens, are of a colder colour, equally fugitive, and are now obsolete.

SCHEELE'S, or SWEDISH GREEN.

Chemical Names and Composition.—Cupric arsenite. Copper and arsenic.

Artistic Qualities.—A good light green when well prepared. Should not be used in flesh tints. Is less opaque and of a darker shade than emerald green (of copper).

Conditions of Permanency.—Similar in stability to emerald green. Permanent when alone and with white lead. Is less affected than the other copper greens by foul air and damp.

Conditions of Non-Permanency.—Is destroyed when mixed with the true Naples yellow or antimoniate of lead.

General Adulterations.—All the metals used in its manufacture are present in a free state if carelessly prepared.

Tests for Purity and Nature of Adulterants.—The presence of free copper and arsenic can be detected by using the tests for those metals.

Remarks.—Since it contains arsenic, it should be carefully kept from children, and the brush should not be put in the mouth.

TERRA VERTE (Green Earth, Verona Green, Green Bice, Verdetta, or Holly Green).

Chemical Names and Composition.—A species of ochre containing silica, oxide of iron, magnesia, potash, and water. When calcined it forms another pigment called Verona brown.

Artistic Qualities.—Grows darker when mixed with oil. Weak in body and semi-transparent, dries well in oil, and is useful for glazing.

Conditions of Permanency.—Is very durable alone and with other colours; strong light and vitiated atmosphere have no effect on it.

Conditions of Non-Permanency.—Its colour is destroyed by acids.

General Adulterations.—Adulterated with yellow ochre.

Tests for Purity and Nature of Adulterants.—See tests given under yellow ochres.

Remarks.—Useful to landscape and marine painters. In combination with Indian red and Naples yellow, it gives a series of mild russet greens, of much use in middle distance.

VERDIGRIS, or Viride Æris.

Chemical Names and Composition.—An acetate of copper crystallised or distilled; a compound from acetous acid and oxide of copper. The verdigris of commerce is a sub-acetate of copper, *i.e.* a salt in which the oxide is in the largest proportion. Burnt verdigris means an oxide instead of an acetate of copper.

Artistic Qualities.—A very bright, cold green: dries rapidly, and is useful for glazing. Before using it for glazing, the colour over which it is laid should be thoroughly dry, or else the whole will crack. Burnt verdigris is of an olive hue, and from its siccative qualities dries admirably. Distilled verdigris is useful for the plumage of birds, panes of church windows, draperies, and where lively greens, as in precious stones, are desirable. New clean brushes should be used with this pigment.

Conditions of Permanency.—Crystallised verdigris, when ground in oil varnish is not soluble in water. In oil it is permanent in light and air, and in varnish stands better than in oil. Verdigris employed as directed by Bouvier undergoes no change:—"It is so imprisoned in the copaiba, which becomes very hard, and in the varnish, which dries instantly, that the air has no time to attack it." Bouvier found that after eighteen years verdigris used after his method was as bright as when first put on.

Conditions of Non-Permanency.—Crystallised verdigris should be varnished as soon as dry, because being a soluble salt it would be carried off whenever the picture is washed. The least durable of copper greens. Light fades it in water. Damp and foul air first bleach it, then turn it black. In oil, moisture and foul air change its colour, and cause it to effloresce or rise to the surface through the oil.

General Adulterations.—Largely adulterated with chalk and sulphate of copper.

Tests for Purity and Nature of Adulterants.—If pure, vinegar will dissolve it, forming a green liquid useful for colouring maps. To test for chalk, see baryta white. If adulterared with sulphate of copper, SH_2 will indicate the sulphur present in it as a brownish black mass of cupric sulphide, which is insoluble in dilute acids.

Remarks.—Bouvier's directions for using verdigris green are these:—

"Carefully finish the object to be glazed by it, using for the greens thereof Prussian blue and Naples yellow or yellow ochre. Keep the colour yellowish, or even on occasion make it pure yellow, but let no white be admitted. . . . Let the object thus painted dry; glaze, then having crushed some crystallised or distilled verdigris into a fine powder, mix into it as quick as possible equal parts of fine mastic varnish and balsam of copaiba (the whitest and least viscous obtainable), then spread this rapidly as a glaze over every part, both light and shade, as if you were varnishing. If the glaze be not deep enough, let it thoroughly dry and then paint afresh."

VIENNA GREEN, or Brunswick or Schweinfurt Green.

Chemical Names and Composition.—Compound obtained from sulphate of copper, white oxide of arsenic, potash, and acetous acid. Ordinary Brunswick green is compounded of chromate of lead and Prussian blue.

Artistic Qualities.—Ordinary Brunswick green cannot be used on walls containing lime, as the action of the latter alters the tint of the Prussian blue in this green.

Conditions of Non-Permanency.—Not likely to be of any permanency.

General Adulterations.—Carelessness of manufacture will leave portions of the constituents in a free state.

Tests for Purity and Nature of Adulterants.—Wash the green with water and dip in a blue litmus paper; it will be turned red if free acid be present, and a red paper will be turned blue if free potash be present. If free copper is present in the solution, a little potassic hydrate will throw down a light blue precipitate.

Remarks.—Ordinary Brunswick green is not suitable for pictures, as the reaction of the chromate of lead on the Prussian blue ultimately destroys it.

VIRIDIAN, or Guignet's Green.

Chemical Names and Composition.—Oxide of chromium, containing a small quantity of water.

Artistic Qualities.—Is eligible in fresco. Is a rich transparent colour; used with aureolin, is a brilliant foliage green, and useful for glazing and for aërial and liquid effects. "A gorgeous green, being not unlike the richest velvet. Pure and clear as the emerald, it may be called the Prussian blue of greens, of such richness, depth, and transparency is it. In hue of a light bluish green, its deepest shades verge on black, while its light tints are marked by transparent clearness unsurpassed. No compound of blue and yellow will afford a green at once so beautiful and stable, so gifted with the quality of light, and therefore so suited for aërial and liquid effects. When fitly compounded, it will be found invaluable for the glassy liquidity of seas, in painting which it becomes incumbent to employ pigments more or less transparent."

Conditions of Permanency.—Is the most permanent and best green of the palette, and is neither injured by nor injures other pigments. Is unaffected by light, damp, or impure air.

Conditions of Non-Permanency.—Cannot be used in enamelling, as the colour, depending on the water of hydration, is destroyed by the strong heat.

General Adulterations.—If adulterated, other chrome greens will be found.

Remarks.—Is suitable for both aqueous and atmospheric effects; of great use in draperies and illumination.

ZINC, or COBALT GREEN (Rinman's Green).

Chemical Names and Composition.—Compounded of zinc and oxides of cobalt.

Artistic Qualities.—Inferior in colour and body to the chrome greens, but it appears to possess more body than any of the other colours made with zinc.

Conditions of Permanency.—Permanent both alone and in combination, and similar to cobalt blue in character. It resists change from oil, light, and foul air.

General Adulterations.—A spurious green would be made up of cobalt blue and a yellow mechanically mixed.

Tests for Purity and Nature of Adulterants.—See tests given under iron pigments.

Remarks.—Moderately bright in tone. "Zinc green" should more properly indicate a cyanide of zinc and iron, obtained by macerating finely-powdered Prussian blue in a strong solution of chloride of zinc.

CHAPTER III.

BLUE PIGMENTS.

ANTWERP, HAARLEM, BERLIN, or MINERAL BLUE.

Chemical Names and Composition.—Ferro-prussiate of alumina. Similar to Prussian blue, with the addition of the earthy base alum.

Artistic Qualities.—Lighter than, and similar in properties to, Prussian blue. Is a rich blue, fascinating to the artist, but should be used with caution.

Conditions of Permanency.—Is more permanent in proportion to the less amount of aluminous base it possesses.

Conditions of Non-Permanency.—Not so permanent as Prussian blue.

General Adulterations.—Ochres and chalky matters.

Tests for Purity and Nature of Adulterants.—Hydrochloric acid will cause effervescence if chalk be present. Distinguished from Prussian blue by possessing a more earthy fracture.

Remarks.—Lighter in colour and greener in tinge than Prussian blue, with less depth.

CÆRULEUM (Cerulian, or Egyptian Blue).

Chemical Names and Composition.—The modern pigment is a stannate of cobalt. Sulphate of lime is sometimes present. The ancient Egyptian blue was artificially made of carbonate of soda 15 parts, powdered flint 20, and cobalt 3.

Artistic Qualities.—Of dense body. Useful as a water colour, in fresco and enamel; appears better as a blue in night-time than in day.

Conditions of Permanency.—Permanent under the influences of heat, light, or atmosphere.

Conditions of Non-Permanency.—Oils are said to injure the delicacy of its tone.

General Adulterations.—A factitious cerulian is obtained by mixing ultramarine with Naples yellow and white lead.

Tests for Purity and Nature of Adulterants.—Test for presence of lead and Naples yellow (which see).

Remarks.—Becomes greenish in time, probably by the yellowing of the oil. Linton says that the ancient cæruleum was a native carbonate of copper.

COBALT BLUE (Cobalt Ultramarine, Vienna Blue, and Azure).

Chemical Names and Composition.—Silicate of cobalt and potassium, or a compound of cobalt and alumina.

Artistic Qualities.—Fine blue pigment. Somewhat deficient in body in water; dries well in oil. Can be used in fresco, enamel, and silicious painting. Useful as a substitute for ultramarine, on account of its brightness of colour, and superior when used in skies and other objects which require even tints. Used occasionally in retrieving the brightness of those tints when too heavy, and in draperies, &c. Capable by its superior brilliancy and contrast of saddening the brightness of other blues.

Conditions of Permanency.—Thoroughly permanent in mixture with other pigments.

Conditions of Non-Permanency.—Light and foul air slightly affect its brilliancy. When not well prepared, some speci mens incline to violet and green.

General Adulterations.—Is purest when free from iron.

Tests for Purity and Nature of Adulterants.—Distinguishable from native and artificial ultramarine by not being discolourable by acids.

Remarks.—Cobalt blues include King's blue (a carbonate of cobalt), Thénard's blue (a salt of cobalt calcined with alumina or oxide of tin), and smalt (a glass coloured with cobalt and then ground).

INDIGO, or Indian Blue.

Chemical Names and Composition.—A vegetable blue.

Artistic Qualities.—Deep blue colour, useful in water and oil. Good body, powerful and transparent; glazes well. Used for twilight and evening skies, but not sufficiently bright for skies on clear days. Is useful for the green of trees when mixed with burnt sienna and gamboge; useful when mixed with lake and gamboge to make greys and neutral tints. Washes smoothly, and much more easily than Prussian blue.

Conditions of Permanency.—Permanent under ordinary conditions of pure atmosphere, &c.

Conditions of Non-Permanency.—Fugitive in tint with white lead, and affected by foul air.

General Adulterations.—Sometimes adulterated 50 per cent. with sand, pulverised slate, or earthy bodies when sold in dust or small pieces.

Tests for Purity and Nature of Adulterants.—The best indigo will swim upon water, and is lightest, brightest, and most copper-coloured, of most fine grain, and inodorous.

Remarks.—Useful to supersede Prussian blue for shadows. Prussian blue with a little black and a tinge of green in it equally replaces indigo in its uses.

PRUSSIAN, BERLIN, PARISIAN BLUE.

Chemical Names and Composition.—Prussiate of iron or ferro-cyanide of iron, *i.e.* it consists of carbon, nitrogen, and iron.

Artistic Qualities.—Good body, powerful yet transparent. Combines well with white lead to form splendid though harsh tints. Dries and glazes well in oil. Imperfectly made, has a greenish tinge. Good drier. Suitable for the blue part of clear fine-weather skies at all times of the day; makes a purple when mixed with lake, which is useful for distant mountains and drapery. Makes a bright green when mixed with gamboge, and is permanent, but rarely used for the greens of trees; makes a good pearly grey for clouds when mixed with lake and a little gamboge.

Conditions of Permanency.—Fairly durable, though less permanent than the blues of cobalt or ultramarine. Soft or distilled water should be used with it in water colours, since any carbonate or lime present in "hard" water will injure its tone.

Conditions of Non-Permanency.—Alkalies decompose it, and strong light causes it to fade, but darkness restores its colour. Hydrochloric acid again restores its colour after action on it of alkalies.

General Adulterations.—Ochres and other earths, mineral matters, chalk, pipeclay, sulphates of lime and baryta; sometimes starch coloured blue with iodine.

Tests for Purity and Nature of Adulterants.—Best kinds are intense, almost black in hue, hard and brittle. Are inodorous and tasteless, and adhere to the tongue. If pure this blue does not effervesce with acids; but if adulterated with carbonates, as chalk, it does effervesce with acids. If starch be present, boiling water renders the pigment pasty.

Remarks.—Cannot be used in fresco or silicious painting, because of action of alkalies. Turnbull's blue (ferro-cyanide of iron) is lighter and more delicate than Prussian blue. A green made with Prussian blue cannot be used on walls containing lime.

SMALT (Azure, Enamel, Dumont's, or Royal Blue).

Chemical Names and Composition.—Is a fused silicate of cobalt, consisting of glass rendered blue by fusion; the glass is then powdered and used as a pigment.

Artistic Qualities.—Is a vivid and gorgeous blue, bright, deep, and transparent. Most valuable for fresco and silicious painting; can be used in water and oil; possesses little body, and does not wash well.

Conditions of Permanency.—Is permanent; not affected by SH_2.

General Adulterations.—The finer it is ground the more it decreases in intensity, until it eventually becomes colourless. Chalk (carbonate of lime) is the most usual adulterant.

Tests for Purity and Nature of Adulterants.—See above test for chalk.

Remarks.—Bouvier says it dries well, Tingry that it is a bad drier. Probably the bad drier was of a coarse variety. One way to use it was to strew it as a dry powder on a freshly-painted blue ground.

ULTRAMARINE (Outremer Lazurline, Lazuline Blue, or Lazurstein).

Chemical Names and Composition.—Lapis lazuli; it consists of silica, alumina, soda, and sulphur.

Artistic Qualities.—Pure in tint, transparent in shade, dries and works well in oil, and from its silicious nature is useful in fresco and silicious painting. Mingles well with blacks, greens, and greys, and reds for purple. **Ultramarine Ash** is obtained from the stone after the richer and more intense blue has been exhausted. Although not equal in beauty and inferior in strength of colour to ultramarine, it is a valuable by-product, varying in shade from light to dark, and in hue from pale azure to cold blue with a grey cast. It affords delicate and extremely tender tints, not so positive as ultramarine, but which, as water colour, washes much better. It furnishes greys softer, purer, and more suited to the pearly tints of flesh, skies, distances, foliages, shadows of drapery, &c., than those composed of other blues, with white and black, which the old masters were wont to employ. Ultramarine, however, produces the same effect when broken with black and white, and is thus sometimes carried throughout the colouring of a picture. The ash, compounded with lampblack, gives a soft cold grey for dark lowering clouds, or for twilight away from the sun's influence. Alone it is adapted to very remote hills or mountains, and with orient yellow or aureolin, to distant mountains.

Conditions of Permanency.—Thoroughly permanent for all usual artistic purposes.

Conditions of Non-Permanency.—Hydrochloric acid, or even a weak acid, like citric acid (lemon juice) decomposes both the native and artificial ultramarine. Any acid pigment, as impurely made Constant white, should not be used with it.

General Adulterations.—Sulphates of baryta and lime.

Tests for Purity and Nature of Adulterants.—Add an acid to the pigment, and if pure its colour will completely disappear, and without effervescence; should it effervesce it indicates the presence of a carbonate of some metal as an adulterant. A hot concentrated solution of alum in water, or strong distilled vinegar, discolours and decomposes artificial ultramarine. Nitric acid will destroy the blue colour, leaving only an earthy yellowish-grey gelatine. If cobalt or Prussian blue be used as adulterants, the acid tests will not affect the ultramarine. SH_2 does not affect indigo blue, but destroys ultramarine, and is a good test.

Remarks.—One of the best permanent pigments of the palette, whether native or artificially produced. Varies in tone and purity from deep to pale blue; also obtained with a greenish violet or rose-colour tinge, according as it has yellow or red oxide of iron mixed with it.

ARTIFICIAL, FRENCH, METZ, GMELIN'S BLUE, FACTITIOUS ULTRAMARINE (or Bleu de Garance, and Outremer de Guimet).

Chemical Names and Composition.—Silicate of alumina and silicate of soda with sulphide of sodium.

Artistic Qualities.—This artificial pigment, when well made, can be safely used in place of the native variety.

Conditions of Permanency. — Permanent. The most desirable are those possessing the most colour.

Conditions of Non-Permanency.—Strong heat turns it to dingy blue, and finally white; like the native variety, it is decomposed by ignition in hydrogen gas.

General Adulterations.—Is as a rule darker and less azure than the native pigment.

Tests for Purity and Nature of Adulterants.—No free sulphur should be present, nor sulphate of soda. To test for latter, wash the ultramarine and add baric chloride, and if this salt is present a cloudy precipitate will be given.

Remarks.—In water it should be used with a gum free from acid. *Blue ash* is the product obtained from the last grinding of the lapis lazuli; the refuse remains furnish *Mineral Grey.* Unstable ultramarine (and the artificial is stable and unstable) blackens with white lead, which the genuine ultramarine does not.

New Blue is an artificial ultramarine, hovering in tint between a rich ultramarine and cobalt.

Permanent Blue is a pale ultramarine with a cobalt hue.

CHAPTER IV.

YELLOW PIGMENTS.

AUREOLIN.

Chemical Names and Composition.—Cobalt yellow : a composition of cobalt, potassium, and oxide of nitrogen.

Artistic Qualities.—A rich, brilliant, transparent colour; mixes easily with other pigments. Useful for oil, water, or fresco. Salter says:—"With white it forms very beautiful and transparent tints. With cobalt and rose madder it forms exceedingly pure and transparent aërial greys. With sepia in addition it forms most agreeable delicate tints for distant trees when under the influence of a soft light or hazy state of the atmosphere. For foliage it imparts the vividness and freshness of nature to every colour with which it is combined."

Conditions of Permanency.—Permanent alone and in combination. Sunlight, damp, impure air, and SH_2 have no effect on it.

Conditions of Non-Permanency.—It is non-permanent in enamel, since heat destroys its colour. A steel spatula should not be used in mixing it with another pigment, especially if it be impure, since the steel would be oxidised by the abstraction of oxygen, thus weakening the stability of the pigment.

General Adulterations.—Most usual adulterants are the chromates of lead or cadmium yellow.

Tests for Purity and Nature of Adulterants.—To test for cadmium see under cadmic sulphides and chromium. Ammonium sulphate forms a black precipitate with salts of cobalt. SH_2 does not precipitate solutions of cobalt salts. If the pigment be heated it assumes an orange red colour, gives off water, and then nitrous fumes, and leaves sesquioxide of cobalt mixed with nitrate of potassium. If tested in blowpipe flame, the borax bead is coloured a bright blue.

Remarks.—Alkalies and SH_2 have affected some impurely made specimens, and with indigo this has been known to be changed into the white indigo. The action is so very slight, and the specimens so few, that it may be considered the most permanent yellow known. Indigo is oxidised or burnt up by admixture with it, the yellow of the aureolin becoming brown.

BARYTA YELLOW (Yellow Ultramarine, or Lemon Yellow).

Chemical Names and Composition.—Neutral chromate of baryta. Composed of chromic acid and barium. This is the true Lemon yellow.

Artistic Qualities.—Useful in high light, and as a glaze over greens. A light wash gives cool sunny greens in distance. Semi-opaque.

Conditions of Permanency.—The only chromate possessing durability; damp, foul air, light, and steel palette knife have no injurious effect on it. Neither has white lead, nor other pigments, either in oil or water. Permanent in fresco and crayons.

General Adulterations.—Sulphates of lead, baryta, and lime.

Tests for Purity and Nature of Adulterants.—Test for the presence of the metals zinc, lead, and calcium.

Remarks.—Opinions differ on the permanency of this pigment.

CADMIUM YELLOW (Cadmia, or Jaune Brillant).

Chemical Names and Composition.—Sulphide of cadmium or cadmic sulphide. 112 equivalents of cadmium, and 32 equivalents of sulphur.

Artistic Qualities.—Is a rich, intense, brilliant orange; useful in fresco and silicious painting. Excellent body and of great power; works and washes well. For gorgeous sunsets this colour is very valuable. With white, especially Chinese white, it forms beautiful tints for the light touches of bright clouds or mountains.

Conditions of Permanency.—With the exception of the chromate, the cadmium yellows are all sulphides, and therefore unaffected by SH_2. Light, air, and impure atmosphere have no effect. Salter finds that cadmium yellow, if pure and devoid of free sulphur, neither injures nor is injured by white lead. If the pigment is doubted, it is best to use zinc white for forming tints. The full deep cadmium is the most stable.

Conditions of Non-Permanency.—With white lead cadmium yellow is unstable. It should not be brought into contact with pigments likely to be affected by sulphur or a steel palette knife. It decomposes emerald green. The pale cadmiums are somewhat unstable. Lemon cadmium is very fugacious. No free sulphur should be present, as it is injurious to other pigments.

General Adulterations.—Orpiment and chromate of lead, iodine yellow and compounds of copper, bismuth, or mercury are added as adulterants.

Tests for Purity and Nature of Adulterants.—Cadmium may be known from yellow orpiment by not being volatilised when heated, and being insoluble in ammonic sulphide. If a black precipitate be given on adding SH_2, the adulterants may be mercury, lead, bismuth, or copper compounds. To distinguish this yellow from copper compounds add SH_2, and if pure it will be unaffected, and will be insoluble in alkaline sulphides, caustic sulphides, or potassic cyanide; insoluble in cold but soluble in hot dilute nitric and hydrochloric acids. Soluble also in dilute sulphuric acid.

Remarks.—The "pale" cadmium is not strictly so, except in comparison with the deep cadmium we have been considering. This pale cadmium is of a full rich brilliant yellow, but less orange than the deep cadmium. The paler the cadmium yellow, the less permanent it is.

CHROME YELLOWS (Jaune Minéral, Cologne Yellow, Pale and Deep Chrome, Orange Chrome, Citron, Leipzig or Paris Yellow).

Chemical Names and Composition.—Chromates of lead, in which the latter metal more or less exists in proportion to the depth or paleness of the pigment; it is chromic acid combined with the metallic base. There are other chrome yellows, being chromates of strontian or zinc, but they are little used on the palette. Mineral yellow is a compound of lead and chlorine. Cologne yellow consists of chromate of lead (25), sulphate of lead (15), and sulphate of lime (60).

Artistic Qualities.—Are of various degrees of depth or tone, from lemon to deep yellow, possessing opacity and good body. Go cordially into tint with white, but they possess a harshness and crudeness when compounded with other colours, and are devoid of that mellow richness which characterises the cadmiums. The action of oils is always too great upon the lead in the presence of oxygen to allow of the colour being quite permanent. They should be used in draperies, where the changing would not greatly matter.

Conditions of Permanency.—The sulphates of baryta and lime are sometimes formed during manufacture, and they are an advantage, in that they not only lend a softness to the colours, but decrease the proportion of lead and the risk of change. Orange chrome is more lasting than yellow chrome. Foul air has no effect on citron yellow.

Conditions of Non-Permanency.—Non-permanent either in strong light, injurious air—in which they blacken—or in tint with white. They are destructive to Prussian and Antwerp blues compounded with them. Are likely to be affected by sulphur compounds and alkalies. The denser the body the more likely are chrome yellows to change. This change is more rapid in water than in oil. Citron yellow in contact with organic substances is apt to turn green.

General Adulterations.—The chromates are often mixed with sulphate of lead—which is white—as well as with the sulphates of baryta and lime. Lead increases the readiness of the chromates to become black in impure air.

Tests for Purity and Nature of Adulterants.—If pure the chrome yellow will be completely dissolved and without effervescence when boiled in a test-tube with a little dilute nitric acid. The borax bead (blowpipe test) will be green if the tested yellow be a chrome yellow. Alkalies, orange or red protochloride of tin, and sulphurous acid reduce Cologne yellow to the metallic state.

Remarks.—Chromate of lead in its natural state was long known as "Siberian Redlead." Cologne yellow is a cheap inferior colour unfit for the palette, but is useful for mixing with other yellows. Jaune minéral is paler than the ordinary chromates of lead. Care should be taken as to what pigments are mixed with these chromates. Sulphides are liable to be acted on by the lead in the chromates.

Cologne Earth.—This colour resembles sepia, but has more depth when dry. It is useful for making sketches, especially strong effects and classical subjects. These can afterwards be coloured, and the Cologne earth gives sobriety without coldness to the various tints which are laid over it.

GAMBOGE (variously written Gamboge, Camboge, Cambogia, Gambodium, Gamboage, &c.).

Chemical Names and Composition.—Vegetable yellow. A resinous gum which distils from various trees of a resinous nature.

Artistic Qualities.—A clear yellow, bright and transparent, readily dissolving in water. Somewhat deficient in light and depth. Dries well, and can safely be used with other pigments. Mixed with lemon yellow of barium, can be used in oil. Useful for greens when mixed with blues, to be used in trees and greens, and to make greys and neutral tints when used with lake and indigo or Prussian blue, but most frequently with indigo. It should not be used in the horizon tints of evening skies, yellow ochre being a more mellow tint and preferable in tone. Gamboge will make a good orange colour when mixed with burnt sienna, useful for autumnal tints or faded trees. Makes pure green when mixed with indigo and Prussian blue.

Conditions of Permanency.—Fairly permanent if properly employed. Mixed with other pigments, from its gum resin, it conduces to their stability and keeps its place well.

Conditions of Non-Permanency.—Impure air deepens, and light weakens its tone. Not so stable in oil as water. White lead and other metallic pigments injure it, terrene and alkaline substances redden it, and alcohol dissolves it and alters its colour.

General Adulterations.—Earthy matters.

Tests for Purity and Nature of Adulterants.—The tests for organic substances are too complex to produce satisfactory results in the hands of an amateur in analysis.

Remarks.—In landscape, gamboge affords, with indigo or Antwerp blue, clear, bright greens, and with sepia a very useful sober tint. For sunsets and sunrise, use gamboge mixed with cadmium yellow.

INDIAN YELLOW (or Purree, or Powre).

Chemical Names and Composition.—Uriophosphate of lime. A magnesian salt of a curious acid called euxanthic.

Artistic Qualities.—Pure yellow. Valuable in water under strong sunlight. Of far greater body than gamboge; can be used in fresco. In oils useful for greens in landscapes. Is very brilliant, and being transparent is useful in glazing over greens which may be too dark and heavy, and to give them richness.

Conditions of Permanency.—Permanent in strong light and foul air. Lime does not affect it, hence useful in fresco.

Conditions of Non-Permanency.—Fugitive in oil, both alone and in tint. Affected by darkness and obscurity. Is injurious to cochineal lakes and carmines; becomes brown by mixture with pigments containing oxygen.

Remarks.—Blackness in the shadows of foliage resulting from too much indigo is best corrected by this pigment employed thickly.

KING'S OR CHINESE YELLOW (Orpiment, or Auripigmentum).

Chemical Names and Composition.—Arsenious sulphide; arsenious or sulpharsenious anhydride, a combination of sulphide and oxide of arsenic. Found natural; also made artificially.

Artistic Qualities.—A fine yellow, of good body. Works well. Highly poisonous.

Conditions of Permanency.—Semi-permanent in oil or water.

Conditions of Non-Permanency.—White lead destroys arsenical yellows. Cannot be used with Naples yellow made from antimoniate of lead. Should not be used with green chromium oxides.

Tests for Purity and Nature of Adulterants.—If pure it will be entirely volatilised when heated on a piece of porcelain; neither should it alter its colour when warmed with dilute hydrochloric acid. Test for white lead.

Remarks.—The sulphur in combination with the arsenic, having less affinity for that metal than for lead, lets it go, and forms a sulphide of lead of a dark greyish colour when this yellow is used with lead paints.

LEMON YELLOW.

Chemical Names and Composition.—Chromate, carbonate, and sulphate of lead. A mixture of chromium, carbon, sulphur, oxygen, and lead.

Artistic Qualities.—It has some better qualities than the chrome yellows generally.

Conditions of Permanency.—Fairly permanent under ordinary conditions when well prepared.

Conditions of Non-Permanency.—Less affected by SH_2 than the chrome yellows.

General Adulterations.—Sulphates of baryta and lime and arsenic.

Tests for Purity and Nature of Adulterants.—Test for the metals barium, calcium, and arsenic.

MASSICOT (or Masticot).

Chemical Names and Composition.—Protoxide of lead. A higher degree of oxidation transforms massicot into minium. Combination of lead and oxygen.

Artistic Qualities.—Unsuitable for fresco. May be employed in preparing the drying oils, but drying oils prepared from lead pigments are dangerous to use. Light yellow sold in shops under this name is generally Ceruse calcined.

Conditions of Permanency.—Pure and unmixed it is as permanent or fugitive as white lead.

Conditions of Non-Permanency.—In tint with white lead, and in damp and foul air, it is destroyed.

General Adulterations.—Other yellows compounded with white.

Tests for Purity and Nature of Adulterants.—Employ blowpipe test for chrome and baryta yellows.

Remarks.—One of the undesirable pigments. All lead pigments, notwithstanding their opacity, good body, and easy working, should be banished from the palette if permanency is desired.

NAPLES YELLOW (the "Giallolino" of the Italians).

Chemical Names and Composition.—Now compounded of zinc; formerly lead oxide and antimony, or antimoniate of lead.

Artistic Qualities.—Good body, opacity, and covering power. The yellow now used in enamel painting is very similar to Naples yellow, being composed of the oxides of antimony and lead.

Conditions of Permanency.—Not affected by sunlight. Prof. Church says that the continental Naples yellow, composed of zinc and antimony, is permanent.

Conditions of Non-Permanency.—Affected by SH_2, foul gases, and steel (which it oxidises by parting with oxygen) or iron pigments, as ochres, Prussian or Antwerp blues.

General Adulterations.—Sulphates of lead, barium, and lime.

Tests for Purity and Nature of Adulterants.—Should be tested for the presence of lead, since that metal if in its composition is very injurious.

Remarks.—In the manufacture of Naples yellow it is of the greatest importance that the metals combined should be in the complete state of oxides.

YELLOW LAKES (Madder Yellow, Italian, English, and Dutch Pink, Quercitron Yellow or Lake).

Chemical Names and Composition.—Vegetable dyes on earthy bases. Obtained from annato, turmeric, and quercitron.

Artistic Qualities.—Bright yellow; very transparent; bad driers in oil. Time changes their colour to orange or foxy hue.

Conditions of Permanency.—Fairly durable if pure.

Conditions of Non-Permanency.—Light, oxygen, and white lead destroy their colour. Metallic, arsenic, and alkaline bodies redden them.

General Adulterations.—If adulterated will be with yellow dyes.

Remarks.—Lakes of all colours should be used with caution and looked upon with suspicion.

YELLOW OCHRES (these include Jaune de Fer, Jaune de Mars, Sienna, or Raw Sienna).

Chemical Names and Composition.—Hydrates of iron, and peroxides of iron; *i.e.* they are composed of oxygen, water, and iron, sometimes closely combined with silica and alumina.

Artistic Qualities.—Semi-opaque in oil or water. Useful for mixing for tints, and with Prussian blue to form greens. When calcined they acquire a deeper colour, sometimes becoming brown and red. Should be heated to 212° before mixing with oil, to expel superfluous moisture. Useful for stone buildings or plaster, cornfields, and yellow lights of the sky towards the horizon; mixes well with Venetian red for warm lights on buildings, &c., but never to be used in the green for greens of trees, since it is not transparent enough, and liable to be washed off too easily. Burnt Sienna is useful for rich banks of earth in sunshine and evening tints, and for glowing tints on buildings; not to be used on the horizon tints of skies, but particularly useful in making greens of various degrees of warmth and depth, when mixed with purple grey; easily converted into different degrees of warm or sober brown. Roman Ochre is useful for the purpose of yellow ochre, but being less bright is adapted for drawings of a deeper tone, and is more useful for the light tints of stone buildings. Not to be used in the green of trees.

Conditions of Permanency.—Fairly permanent. Foul air does not affect them. The chemically prepared ochres have a more violent action on other pigments than the native variety, and are less preferable.

Conditions of Non-Permanency.—The ochres should not be used with pigments affected by iron, or with carmine, lake, and intense blue. They affect sulphates of lead.

General Adulterations.—Chalk and china clay (kaolin). The greater the proportion of clay the brighter the colour. Turmeric, Indian yellow, and yellow of coal-tar colours.

Tests for Purity and Nature of Adulterants.—Hydrochloric acid will cause effervescence if chalk be present. Boil this solution, and if clay be present it will exhibit itself as a white gelatinous residue. When there is a proportion of clay the substance feels greasy, and has more body than one mixed with chalk. Wash with ammonia; if coal-tar yellow be present the liquid is coloured.

Remarks.—Jaune de Mars and Jaune de Fer are artificially prepared iron ochres. Merimée gives good reasons for considering that no artificial ochres can have the same permanency as natural ochres.

Mars Orange is a subdued orange of the burnt sienna class, but without the brown tinge that distinguishes the latter. It is marked by special clearness and purity of tone with much transparency; it affords bright sunny tints in its pale washes and combines effectively with white. Being an artificial iron ochre, it is more chemically active than native ochres, and needs to be cautiously employed with pigments affected by iron, such as the lakes of cochineal, and intense blue.

Mars Yellow, or **Jaune de Mars**, **Jaune de Fer**, **Iron Yellow**, **&c.**, is an artificially prepared iron ochre of the nature of sienna earth. In its general qualities it resembles the ochres, with the same eligibility and exceptions; but is more transparent, as well as purer, clearer, and richer and brighter. Like them it is quite permanent.

Orient Yellow is absolutely permanent and perfectly unexceptionable in all respects, both in water and oil. It equals aureolin in stability; not possessed of the same amount of transparency, it is distinguished by greater richness and depth. Of a soft golden hue, lustrous and luminous, it resembles a brilliant and somewhat opaque Indian yellow. A gorgeous and durable substitute for that fugitive pigment is produced by compounding the orient with aureolin, or by using the latter as a glaze. Being more transparent than the cadmiums, and less obtrusive, this yellow is adapted, for mellow sunset and sunrise clouds, as for instance, sunshine on distant mountains. With French blue it affords a beautiful sea-green, and, mixed with aureolin, gives fine green tints. It is also eligible for draperies and illumination. For enamelling it is inadmissible, the colour being destroyed by great heat; but in fresco it may be safely employed.

Turner Yellow, Cassel Yellow, Montpellier Yellow, Vienna Yellow, Mineral Yellow.—These various names belong to quite a number of colours, the composition of which is not properly established. Nevertheless they appear to result from the combination of a protochloride of lead with variable proportions of oxide of lead, and consequently suffer the disadvantages of lead pigments.

CHAPTER V.

RED PIGMENTS.

CADMIUM RED.

Chemical Names and Composition.—Is a simple original pigment containing no base but cadmium.

Artistic Qualities.—Approaches an orange scarlet tone; has great depth; works and dries well. Gives delicate washes, and is useful where opacity is undesirable.

Conditions of Permanency.—Mixes readily and safely with other colours. Not affected by light, impure air, or exposure to atmosphere.

Conditions of Non-Permanency.—Must not be used for enamel painting.

General Adulterations.—If adulterated will be with red lead or vermilion.

Tests for Purity and Nature of Adulterants.—Test for lead. Boil in water, and add SH_2 to solution. A dark precipitate indicates lead. To test for vermilion, heat a little in test-tube; the mercury will volatilise and condense in metallic globules on sides of tube.

Remarks.—Useful for all kinds of work but enamel. Compounded with white, this red yields a series of fine flesh tints.

CHINESE VERMILION, or Carmine Vermilion.

Chemical Names and Composition.—This pigment was sometimes a sulphide of arsenic, but is now obtained from mercury.

Artistic Qualities.—Has a somewhat crimson hue not at all inclined to orange. Mixed with white is useful for rose and lilac tints of some complexions.

Conditions of Permanency.—Safe to use with madder lakes.

Conditions of Non-Permanency.—Unsafe in combination with the lakes of cochineal.

General Adulterations.—See Vermilion.

Tests for Purity and Nature of Adulterants.—Same as for vermilion.

Remarks.—Scarlet and extract of vermilion are synonymous terms. Orange vermilion gives delicate carnations, and is durable in oil and water.

CRIMSON LAKE.

Chemical Names and Composition.—Is an extract from the "coccus cacti" insect fixed to oxide of iron or aluminous base, and contains more of this aluminous base than carmine does. The colour of this lake should be imparted to it during the process of manufacture, and not by subsequent mechanical mixture.

Artistic Qualities.—Not so deep nor brilliant as carmine. More useful in water than in oil, and useful for glazing; over vermilion it produces a most brilliant scarlet, but is apt to vanish therefrom. Poppy oil is the best vehicle to use with cochineal lakes.

Conditions of Permanency.—More valuable and durable in water than in oil.

Conditions of Non-Permanency.—Unstable either alone or in combination. Strong light renders crimson lake fugacious, whether in water or in oil; white lead and other lead pigments, Naples yellow, and arsenical colours, destroy its hue. Lakes mixed with linseed oil turn livery.

General Adulterations.—If made from an inferior insect, heavy spar, carbonate of lead, and Venice talc are sometimes added to give it the silvery-grey reflection that is always to be met with on the best insect. Logwood and chalk are also sometimes added.

Tests for Purity and Nature of Adulterants.—A solution of ammonia will purple the lakes made with logwood, Brazil wood, and others, but will not dissolve the colours produced from them. To distinguish other adulterants, use the respective tests for chalk, heavy spar, carbonate of lead, &c., given under white lead.

Remarks.—Gives richness in flower painting and in illumination. It forms excellent greys with cobalt and gamboge, and as a foreground colour it should be mixed with Vandyke brown. Useless for frescoes, as alkaline bodies purple the tones of lakes. A cochineal lake.

CARMINE LAKE.

Chemical Names and Composition.—A cochineal lake.

Artistic Qualities.—Has great power in full touches; possesses clearness in the pale washes; works well. Seldom used in landscape painting.

Conditions of Permanency.—Carmine, containing less base

and most colouring matter, is the most permanent of the cochineal lakes. Oil or varnish as vehicles protect it. Impure air has little effect on it.

Conditions of Non-Permanency.—In glazing, strong light causes the glaze to vanish, and in tint with white lead it is fugacious.

General Adulterations.—Starch, vermilion, and alumina are occasionally added as adulterants.

Tests for Purity and Nature of Adulterants.—These may be detected by the tests given for cochineal lakes in general, or by adding liquid ammonia and then heating. The colouring matter is entirely dissolved, while the impurities remain insoluble.

Remarks.—The name was formerly confined to the fine fæculences of the Kermes and cochineal tinctures, but now includes any pigment which is like them in beauty and powdery texture (as blue carmines), though the term is usually confined to crimson and scarlet lakes of cochineal.

INDIAN LAKE, or Lac Lake.

Chemical Names and Composition.—A resinous secretion of the "coccus ficus" deposited on twigs and branches of plants.

Artistic Qualities.—Is a good deep colour, hard and nearly transparent.

Conditions of Permanency.—Used thickly or in strong glazing, as a shadow colour, it is of great body and much permanence. (Salter.)

Conditions of Non-Permanency.—Not thoroughly permanent, but still more so than the other cochineal lakes. Is fugitive with white lead and in thin glazing.

General Adulterations.—The most usual are chalk and sulphate of lime (plaster of Paris) and silica.

Tests for Purity and Nature of Adulterants.—The native variety has a brilliant conchoidal fracture.

Remarks.—Inferior in brilliancy and durability to madder lakes.

INDIAN RED and PERSIAN RED.

Chemical Names and Composition.—Indian red is a hematite or peroxide of iron containing oxygen, iron, and earthy matters. Besides the Persian red obtained from the ochres, there is another which is a chromate of lead.

Artistic Qualities.—Indian red has good body, of a purple russet hue, and is useful for fresco and silicious painting provided lime is not present. Goes well into combination.

Conditions of Permanency.—Permanent.

Conditions of Non-Permanency.—Contains much oxygen, and when mixed with lakes and pigments, abstracting oxygen, its stability is weakened.

General Adulterations—Chromates of lead and red ochres.

Tests for Purity and Nature of Adulterants.—To distinguish Persian red from other reds, if pounded in a mortar it assumes an orange hue. To test for chromates of lead use SH_2.

Remarks.—Persian red is sometimes used to adulterate vermilion, light and other reds. Chromate of lead in its natural state was known as Siberian red lead.

IODINE SCARLET, or Iodide of Mercury.

Chemical Names and Composition.—Iodide of mercury or mercuric iodide. 200 equivalents of mercury and 254 equivalents of iodine.

Artistic Qualities.—Good body and opacity. A magnificent scarlet, unequalled by any other pigment.

Conditions of Non-Permanency.—Not permanent. It is subject to evanescence by slight influences. Is easily decomposed by other pigments; pure atmosphere renders its colour fugacious; foul air destroys its scarlet hue; light causes it to vanish.

General Adulterations.—Many adulterants which affect its hue.

Tests for Purity and Nature of Adulterants.—The best quality is of the finest colour. Soluble in alcohol and in excess of potassic iodide.

Remarks.—Although useless as a pigment, it is mentioned here that its employment may be guarded against.

MADDER LAKES (Madder Carmine or Tinted Carmine, Pink Madder, Rose Rubiate or Liquid Madder, Lake or Rose Madder).

Chemical Names and Composition.—These lakes are extracted from the root of the "Rubia Tinctorum."

Artistic Qualities.—*Brown and Purple Madder Lakes* are useful in landscapes for cattle, draperies and mossy stones, and thatch near the foreground. *Madder Carmine* is the richest and deepest, and contains more colouring matter than base. It varies in hue according to the mode of preparation. *Madder Lake,* useful for purples when mixed with indigo and Prussian blue; the last should be used principally for distant hills and mountains. This mixture is also useful for the shadows of nearer but not yet distant hills. It makes a grey or neutral tint when mixed with gamboge and Prussian blue or cobalt. Madder lake is bright, rubs up easily, and with a better body of colour than the bright madders of cochineal, and lies more evenly. May be mixed with yellow ochre for the warm tint of skies instead of Venetian red. *Pink Madder* is a weaker preparation of this, paler in hue, and possessing less colour. *Rose Madder* is not as intense as madder carmine. It gives the most perfect carnation tints known. Does not rapidly dry in oil; is less easy to work in water than cochineal. With cadmium yellow and Chinese white it is invaluable for glazing. The red portion of a sunset sky may be improved with a thin wash of this pigment. *Rose Rubiate* is a concentrated tincture of a beautiful and perfect rose-colour and transparency. In its simple state it is used as a water colour with or without gum. In oil it dries by acting as a siccative.

Conditions of Permanency.—Madder lakes are the only thoroughly permanen tlakes of the palette. Madder carmine is the only desirable carmine for painting in oil or water.

Conditions of Non-Permanency.—When adulterated their permanency is affected in respect of the nature of the adulterations used.

General Adulterations.—Madders are often adulterated with brickdust, red ochre, red sand, clay, mahogany sawdust, logwood, sandal and Japan wood, and bran; whilst the French madders have gum, sugar, salts, and other soluble bodies, as likewise lac, cochineal, and carthamus or safflower.

Tests for Purity and Nature of Adulterants.—Liquid ammonia or alkalies generally dissolve the colours of cochineal, lac, and safflower, so their detection is easy. If the liquid remains uncoloured on adding ammonia to an assumed madder lake, in all probability the pigment is genuine.

Remarks.—"Lake" is a term applied either to red, yellow, or blue pigments formed by precipitating colouring matters, as tinctures, on to some metallic oxide, alumina or other earth. All vegetable lakes should be regarded with suspicion if used in thinning, glazing, or delicate flesh or sky tints. Pink madder is now almost obsolete; the name is given to rose madder, which is also called madder lake. In using these lakes a little of the dry colour should be crushed with the muller and made up into a thick paste with a few drops of poppy oil, drying oil being used to thin it as it is wanted for use. By thus omitting the drying oil the pigment will remain moist for days.

RED LEAD (Minium, or Saturnine Red).

Chemical Names and Composition.—An oxide of lead. It is generally a mixture of two oxides of lead not chemically compounded, and is of an uncertain composition.

Artistic Qualities.—Of a scarlet colour, heavy and opaque in body. Is an excellent drier with other colours, but being lead it cannot be safely employed except with the ochres, earths, and blacks in general.

Conditions of Permanency.—When pure or alone it is not

affected by light, and in simple varnish or oil not rendered drying by any metallic oxide it may stand a long time under favourable circumstances.

Conditions of Non-Permanency.—White lead destroys its colour. SH_2 blackens it, and when mixed with it red lead undergoes a rapid oxidation. Nitric acid turns it brown. Red lead follows white lead in saponifying with the oil, and so in time loses its opacity, and allows the background to appear through.

General Adulterations.—Badly made red lead is of a brownish colour.

Tests for Purity and Nature of Adulterants.—To distinguish red lead from vermilion or iron reds (as the ochres) add a solution of SH_2 and a black precipitate of lead sulphide will indicate the leaden nature of the pigment.

Remarks.—Altogether unsuitable for the artist's palette.

RED OCHRE (Indian Ochre, Scarlet Ochre, or Light Red).

Chemical Names and Composition.—Is usually a sulphate of iron calcined into an oxide. Sometimes it is one of the yellow oxides of iron calcined.

Artistic Qualities.—It is less harsh to the eye than vermilion, and more harmonious in certain combinations.

Conditions of Permanency.—The ochres are permanent when well prepared. Should not be mixed with those pigments likely to be affected by iron.

Conditions of Non-Permanency.—Should sulphate of lime be present, it is unsuitable for silicious painting, since silicate of lime is formed by union with the silicate of potash, and the pigments become hard and lumpy.

General Adulterations.—The native pigment is mixed with earthy substances.

Remarks.—With vermilion or madder lake it is useful for the shadows of light red draperies.

RED ORPIMENT, or Realgar.

Chemical Names and Composition.—Diarsenious disulphide; *i.e.* a compound of arsenic and sulphur.

Artistic Qualities.—Red orpiment, which is an orange colour, contains most arsenic, whereas yellow orpiment contains most sulphur. Poisonous.

Conditions of Non-Permanency.—A dangerous body to use, since it destroys other pigments and absorbs the colour of the ground, especially so if the latter contain lead.

Tests for Purity and Nature of Adulterants.—Arsenic is volatilised like the mercury in vermilion when heated in a narrow test-tube, and only a small portion of the realgar should be used. This arsenic pigment gives off an odour similar to garlic when heated in a test-tube.

Remarks.—Both this pigment and its well-known yellow companion should be excluded from the palette.

VENETIAN, ENGLISH, or PRUSSIAN RED, or Scarlet Ochre.

Chemical Names and Composition.—An oxide obtained from iron. Prepared by calcining sulphate of iron, to which a little nitric acid may be advantageously added. The result is a peroxide of iron more powerful and of a more scarlet tone than light red.

Artistic Qualities.—With cobalt or French blue, with which it mixes well, it gives fine pearly greys. Heightened in tone by admixture with madder lake. Saddened by black, it gives low-toned reds useful for buildings. Compounded with aureolin, yields a clear orange. Useful for the red horizon tints of skies, and to make a neutral tint when mixed with indigo and a very little lake, and is most excellent for its quality of mixing well with all colours (Indian ink not excepted), and lying evenly and smoothly on the paper, with less trouble than light red, for which it is a valuable substitute. It is preferable to indigo red, which is too heavy and purple, and is very good to mix with yellow ochre for general tints used in bricks, tiles, &c.

Conditions of Permanency.—When well prepared it is permanent, but since it contains iron it should not be mixed with pigments affected by that metal. It is apparently not affected by SH_2, light, damp, or foul air.

Conditions of Non-Permanency.—Sometimes unsuitable for silicious painting (see red ochre).

General Adulterations.—In the manufacture of Venetian red, lime sometimes becomes mixed with it, and as the pigment is made from the sulphate of iron, sulphate of lime is formed. The presence of this impurity prevents the use of Venetian red in silicious painting.

Tests for Purity and Nature of Adulterants.—Test for presence of alumina, chalk, and gypsum. If pure no reaction will take place with the tests. Hydrochloric acid completely dissolves pure oxide of iron.

Remarks.—A good all-round pigment.

VERMILION (also called Cinnabar).

Chemical Name and Composition.—Sulphide of mercury. Is obtained native, or is produced artificially by heating together 200 equivalents of mercury with 32 equivalents of sulphur.

Artistic Qualities.—Has good body, due to its opacity; is useful in oil, water, and fresco. It must not be used with iodine, since it does not dry quickly. Compounded with whites, it forms delicate flesh tints, and with cobalt or French blue and white tender aërial greys. This is the brightest of reds; is useful in flesh and drapery, and in painted objects, such as flags, boats, &c., being of that degree of brightness which will, by contrast, send back many other reds into distances.

Conditions of Permanency.—Permanent under all ordinary conditions. Being a sulphide, it is unaffected by SH_2, and should not be brought into contact with a pigment on which sulphur acts injuriously. Vermilion in the course of time turns slightly brown.

Conditions of Non-Permanency.—When heated to a very high temperature with compounds of tin, iron, and antimony, it is decomposed. Unfitted for enamel painting, since alkalies and alkaline carbonates decompose it when at a red heat. Unstable with lakes. Becomes denser with age.

General Adulterations.—Red lead, brickdust, oxide of iron, or Persian red (a peculiar chromate of lead). Sometimes iodine scarlet is added to give extraordinary brilliancy.

Tests for Purity and Nature of Adulterants.—If pure will

be decomposed into metallic mercury and sulphur, and dissipated, when heated in test-tube. Hydrochloric acid and caustic alkalies do not affect it. Oxide of iron may be detected by hydrochloric acid. If lead be present a metallic bead of it will be formed if vermilion be fused on charcoal with carbonate of soda, the metallic mercury passing off as a vapour. If brickdust be present, heat the pigment in long narrow tube: the mercury will volatilise and brickdust remain at the bottom of the tube. Iodine is dissolved by carbon disulphide, which assumes a fine violet colour.

Remarks.—Field's orange vermilion is less opaque and also brighter, clearer, and purer than the ordinary vermilion. Scarlet vermilion possesses a more scarlet hue than vermilion proper.

Mars Red, or Rouge de Mars, is an artificial iron ochre, similar in subdued tint and permanence to the native umber. Its chemical affinities, however, are greater than those of the latter, and it therefore requires to be employed cautiously with pigments affected by iron. In this respect the red resembles its compeers—Mars-yellow, orange, violet and brown—all of which are iron ochres artificially prepared. Possessing the richness and depth of Indian red, it is distinguished by a russet orange hue of light red. Its pale washes are marked by considerable clearness.

Purple Lake is a species of crimson lake with a purple cast, transparent and deep toned and useful in shadows; in other respects resembling that pigment. More durable than crimson lakes.

CHAPTER VI.

BROWN AND BLACK PIGMENTS.

ASPHALTUM or BITUMEN (Antwerp Brown, or Bitumen Judaicum).

Chemical Names and Composition.—A mineral pitch of resin. The native asphalt is non-secure; the artificial is the residue of various resins and bituminous matters distilled for the sake of their essential oils.

Artistic Qualities.—Is a rich brown. Has a powerful body, but is useless, as it liquefies and cracks unless mixed with an unctuous vehicle. It is dissolved in oil of turpentine. The native is superior to the artificial asphaltum when it is used as a permanent brown in water.

Conditions of Non-Permanency.—Is a most destructive pigment, since it contracts and cracks by atmospheric and caloric changes.

General Adulterations.—Asphaltum is often adulterated with foreign matters, all of which render it still more destructive in use.

Tests for Purity and Nature of Adulterants.—If pure it should present a glossy fracture, smooth and nearly black and brilliant. This fracture also has the appearance of undulations, arising, in fact, from the movement it experienced, whilst yet liquid, on the surface of the sea, and in its concrete state it retains this form.

Remarks.—The solution of asphalte in turpentine is commonly called "asphaltum," and the mixture with drying oils "bitumen." Liquid asphaltum is a preparation made for use in water colours.

BISTRE.

Chemical Names and Composition.—The finer parts of beechwood soot extracted by a watery solution.

Artistic Qualities.—Not used in oil, as it dries with difficulty therein; only in water. It has a powerful citrine brown colour, and washes well.

Conditions of Permanency.—A permanent colour.

Conditions of Non-Permanency.—It attracts moisture from the atmosphere, and is therefore liable to engender mildew in water colours.

General Adulterations.—Accidental impurities, as coarse particles of soot, wood-ashes, &c.

Tests for Purity and Nature of Adulterants.—A gritty solution will at once show these impurities.

Remarks.—Used in water like China ink, and has the same effect as brown pink has in oil.

BROWN PINK.

Chemical Names and Composition.—A vegetable lake made from dye woods and French berries by precipitation with alum.

Artistic Qualities.—Great depth and transparency in water colour. All berry varieties dry badly. Works well both in water and in oil.

Conditions of Permanency.—More permanent when worked

in full body than in thin glazings. The quercitron bark variety is semi-stable.

Conditions of Non-Permanency.—When in combination with white lead it fades. The berry variety is fugitive.

General Adulterations.—May accidentally possess an excess of soda or potash from careless manufacture.

Tests for Purity and Nature of Adulterants.—If the alkali be in excess, the pigment possesses a brown hue instead of that of a citron hue.

Remarks.—Should be used carefully in combination. Produces fine greens with Prussian or indigo blue.

BLUE or FRANKFURT BLACK.

Chemical Names and Composition.—Charcoal and calcined Prussian blue; also burnt vine-twigs, cocoanut shells, &c.

Artistic Qualities.—A most useful colour, and dries well in oil. In mixture with white, produces bluish tints.

Conditions of Permanency.—Permanent.

General Adulterations.—Common black mixed with blues.

Tests for Purity and Nature of Adulterants.—It should be free from lumps and of fine texture.

Remarks.—The blue-black of the ancients was made from the lees of wine.

INDIAN INK and CHINESE INK.

Chemical Names and Composition.—Shell-lac 10 parts, borax 20 parts, lampblack and water 40 parts. Chinese ink is the finest lampblack mixed with the oil of sesame and a little camphor.

Artistic Qualities.—Finely opaque in body. When dry on the paper will not yield to the action of water, owing to its combining with the components of the paper.

Conditions of Permanency.—It is thoroughly permanent.

General Adulterations.—Earthy matters and inferior soots.

Tests for Purity and Nature of Adulterants.—Is homogeneous when rubbed in water. When diluted with much water will leave no precipitate after evaporation. When dry its surface is covered with a pellicle of a metallic appearance.

Remarks.—Chinese ink may be distinguished by its being dissolved in vinegar without any precipitate.

LAMPBLACK, or Lamblack.

Chemical Names and Composition.—Smoke black. It is a pure vegetable carbon of fine texture, obtained by burning resins or resinous woods, turpentine, or camphor; or made from the imperfect combustion of bone, oil, coal-tar, and the products of the petroleum stills.

Artistic Qualities.—Is not so intense nor so transparent as ivory black but less brown in its pale tones. It has a very strong body which covers every underlay of colour; works well; it dries badly, but unites well in oil. Since it is a dense solid colour, it must be used sparingly.

Conditions of Permanency.—It is durable.

General Adulterations.—Inferior soot and earthy matters.

Tests for Purity and Nature of Adulterants.—Lampblack is intense in colour and of light weight, the black obtained from coal-smoke being much heavier and coarser; it contains a large quantity of ammonia.

Remarks.—Salter says:—"Mixed with French blue or

cobalt it gives good cloudy greys. With light red and cobalt in different proportions it yields most serviceable silvery tones. In the dark marking of murky and dirty clouds, a compound of lampblack and light red is particularly suited, while a mixture of it with cobalt and purple madder is adapted for slate-coloured sunset and sunrise clouds. In seas the colour is useful with raw sienna."

MANGANESE BROWN.

Chemical Names and Composition.—A deuteroxide of manganese. A native product.

Artistic Qualities.—A useful semi-opaque colour; has such good drying powers that it is often used as a siccative for oils and dark pigments.

Conditions of Permanency.—Quite durable in water and oils.

Conditions of Non-Permanency.—Organic matters decompose manganates, so this should be used cautiously in presence of animal and vegetable lakes.]

General Adulterations.—Various kinds of earths.

Tests for Purity and Nature of Adulterants.—Heated in outer flame (blowpipe test) the borax bead is of an amethyst colour; in inner or reducing flame this bead becomes colourless. This test distinguishes manganese brown from other browns.

Remarks.—The peroxide of manganese forms the manganese black.

MUMMY or EGYPTIAN BROWN.

Chemical Names and Composition.—White pitch and myrrh combined with animal matter.

Artistic Qualities.—A rich transparent colour.

Conditions of Permanency.—It is less liable to crack and move on the canvas than asphaltum.

Conditions of Non-Permanency.—It is a substance better rejected from the palette, as no reliance can be placed on it.

General Adulterations.—Its organic origin renders it liable to contain ammonia and particles of fat in a concrete state, which are undesirable.

Remarks.—Bodies were embalmed 3,000 years ago in liquid bitumen. It is this bitumen, combined with parts of the body, that compose mummy brown.

PRUSSIAN BROWN, or Iron Brown.

Chemical Names and Composition.—Calcined Prussian blue, or an iron oxide with alumina. French Prussian blue, as it contains more alumina, is better than the English Prussian blue.

Artistic Qualities.—It is of great transparency, of a most harmonious tone, and dries well. When asphaltum would be used this should replace it. As good in water as in oil. Produces fine glazes with burnt sienna.

Conditions of Permanency.—Perfectly permanent, and undergoes no change.

General Adulterations.—Harmful chemical constituents are liable to be present from careless manufacture. The iron browns vary in colour according to method of, or carelessness in, preparation.

Tests for Purity and Nature of Adulterants.—The brown made from the English Prussian blue is of a golden yellowish brown. Another Prussian brown, a ferro-cyanide of copper, can be detected by SH_2 and is totally destroyed by the alkaline solutions used in picture-cleaning.

Remarks.—If the calcination of Prussian blue be carried on in closed vessels, a deep black is procured possessing the properties of this brown. The copper Prussian brown is of a rich chocolate colour.

SEPIA.

Chemical Names and Composition.—Extract of cuttle-fish. Consisting of carbonaceous particles and animal gelatine.

Artistic Qualities.—A dusky brown and transparent colour, dries badly in oil.

Conditions of Permanency.—Permanent in oil and water.

General Adulterations.—Earthy particles may be present.

Tests for Purity and Nature of Adulterants.—The pure sepia should be free from gritty particles when dissolved in water.

Remarks.—Very pleasant working colour.

UMBER, RAW and BURNT.

Chemical Names and Composition.—A native ore of iron and manganese, mixed with silex and alumina. Also artificially made.

Artistic Qualities.—Possesses strong drying powers, works and washes well in water. Eligible in fresco, and has good body. Is useful as shadows to warm tints of earth and burnt sienna, and near foregrounds, and for the colour of earth. Useful also for small dark touches of shadow to pebbles, &c., in foreground.

Conditions of Permanency.—Durable in oil and water; grows darker with age.

General Adulterations.—Ochreous or earthy matters, or a too great preponderance of some one of its constituents in a free state.

Tests for Purity and Nature of Adulterants.—Browns are best when deep, rich, and transparent.

Remarks.—An olive brown colour, useful both raw and calcined. Should be used with white and other colours to form greys.

VANDYKE, CAPPAH, RUBENS, CASSEL, and COLOGNE BROWN.

Chemical Names and Composition.—Cappah is a manganese peat. Rubens brown is a native earth of an ochreous character. Cassel brown is a native earthy brown. Cologne brown is an ochreous deep violaceous earth.

Artistic Qualities.—A deep semi-transparent colour, good for glazing. Cassel earth compounded with burnt lake and a little Prussian blue gives a profound black.

Conditions of Permanency.—Nearly permanent. To compensate for the action of strong light, should be mixed with permanent colours, such as umber, Chinese black, and oxide of iron.

Conditions of Non-Permanency.—Strong light affects them. Cologne brown is fugacious.

General Adulterations.—From their earthy nature these browns are liable to possess an unwonted quantity of much undesirable substance.

Tests for Purity and Nature of Adulterants.—The methods of distinguishing these browns, or separating these earthy matters, are too complex for ordinary practice.

Remarks.—All peaty browns, probably from their vegetable colouring, have a slight tendency to become paler when washed very thinly. Use the strongest drying oils with them.

Mars Brown, or Brun de Mars, is either a natural or artificial ochre, containing iron, or iron and manganese; of much richness and strict permanence. It resembles raw umber in being a brown with a citrine cast, but is generally marked by a flash of orange which is not observable in the latter pigment.

Mineral Gray * is obtained from the lapis lazuli, after the refuse and ash has been worked out. It is a pigment peculiar to oil paints; it is admirably adapted to that gray semi-neutrality prevalent in nature in atmospheres. In misty mornings, cloudy skies, and the like, this gray will be found useful.

Neutral Tint is a compound shadow colour of a cool character. It is permanent except that, on exposure, the gray is apt to become grey—a change which may be prevented by a slight addition of ultramarine ash. So protected, it becomes serviceable in landscape for the extreme distance, which, it may be laid down as a general principle, should be painted rather cold than otherwise.

Payne's Gray resembles neutral tint in being a compound colour, and liable to assume a grey cast by time, but differs from it in having more lilac in its hue, and being, therefore,

* Grey is a grey compounded with black and white; gray is a gray with the blue replacing the black.

of a warmer tone. Giving by itself a clear violet shadow, it may be rendered more neutral by a small portion of burnt sienna, an admixture which, whether the gray or sienna predominates, affords useful tints. Compounded with light red or Vandyke brown, the gray is good for shipping and sails or the stems and branches of trees, while, with gamboge or aureolin, it is suited to glossy leaves in high lights, also to vary cold tones in foreground, herbage, &c. Yellow ochre, light red, and Payne's gray form a mixture for banks and roads; the gray ochre and sepia, a most beautiful tint for stones; and brown madder and the gray a fine shade for the black heads and feet of cattle. Alone the gray is serviceable for slates, and, compounded with light red, for bricks or tiles in shadow.

Rubens Madder, otherwise known as Orange Russet, Russet Rubiate, or Field's Russet. This is a very rich crimson russet with a flash of orange; pure, transparent, and of a madder hue between orange and purple. It is a good glazing colour; its thin washes afford fine flesh tints in water; and, as an oil pigment, it dries indifferently and requires to be forced by the addition of a little gold-size or varnish. It is not subject to change by light, time, or mixture of other pigments.

TABLE OF REFERENCE.

Egyptian b. (see cæruleum)
Factitious Ultramarine (see art. ult.)
French b. (see ditto)
Gmelin's b. (see ditto)
Haarlem b. (see Antwerp b.)
Indian b. (see indigo)
Indigo
Lazurline (see ultramarine)
Metz b. (see artificial ultramarine)
Mineral b. (see Antwerp b.)
Mineral Grey (see artificial ult.)
New Blue
Outremer (see ultramarine)
Outremer de Guimet (see art. ult.)
Parisian b. (see Prussian b.)
Permanent Blue
Prussian b.
Royal b. (see smalt)
Smalt
Thénard's b. (see cobalt b.)
Turnbull's b. (see Prussian b.)
Ultramarine
Vienna b. (see cobalt b.)

YELLOW PIGMENTS.

Aureolin
Cobalt y. (see aureolin)
Auripigmentum (see king's y.)
Baryta y.
Camboge (see Gamboge)
Cadmia (see cadmium y.)
Chinese y. (see king's y.)
Citron y. (see chrome ys.)
Cologne y. (see ditto)
Deep Chrome (see ditto)
Dutch Pink (see yellow lakes)
English Pink (see ditto)
Gamboge
Gamboage } (see Gamboge)
Gambodium } (see Gamboge)
Giallolino (see Naples y.)
Indian y.
Italian Pink (see yellow lakes)
Jaune Brillant (see cadmium y.)
Jaune de Fer (see yellow ochres)
Jaune de Mars (see ditto)
Jaune Minéral (see chrome ys.)
King's y.
Leipzig y. (see chrome ys.)
Lemon y. (see baryta y.)
Mars Orange
Mars Yellow
Madder y. (see yellow lakes)
Masticot (see massicot)
Naples y.
Orange chrome (see chrome ys.)
Orient Yellow
Orpiment (see king's y.)
Pale Chrome (see chrome ys.)
Paris y. (see ditto)
Powre or Purree (see Indian y.)
Quercitron y. or lake (see y. lakes)
Raw Sienna (see yellow ochres)
Siberian Red Lead (see chrome ys.)
Sienna (see yellow ochres)
Turner Yellow
Yellow Ultramarine (see baryta y.)

RED PIGMENTS.

Cadmium r.
Carmine Lake
Carmine Vermilion (see Chinese v.)
Chinese Vermilion
Cinnabar (see vermilion)
Crimson Lake
English r. (see Venetian r.)
Field's Orange Ver. (see vermilion)
Indian Lake
Indian Ochre (see red ochre)
Indian r.
Iodine Scarlet
Iodide of Mercury (see iodine s.)
Lac Lake (see Indian lake)
Light r. (see red ochre)
Liquid Madder (see madder lakes)
Mars Red
Madder Carmine (see madder lakes)
Minium (see red lead)
Pink madder (see madder lakes)
Persian r. (see Indian r.)
Purple Lake
Prussian r. (see Venetian r.)
Realgar (see red orpiment)
Red Orpiment
Rose Madder (see madder lakes)
Saturnine r.

Scarlet Ochre (see Venetian r.)
Scarlet Vermilion (see vermilion)
Tinted Carmine (see madder lakes)
Venetian r.
Vermilion

BROWN AND BLACK PIGMENTS.

Antwerp Brown (see asphaltum)
Asphaltum
Blue Black
Bistre
Brown Pink
Bitumen (see asphaltum)
Bitumen Judaicum (see ditto)
Burnt Umber (see umber)
Cappah Brown (see Vandyke b.)
Cassel Brown (see ditto.)
Chinese Ink (see Indian ink)
Cologne Brown
Egyptian Brown (see mummy b.)
Frankfurt Black (see blue black)
Indian Ink
Iron Brown (see Prussian brown)
Lamblack (see lampblack)
Mars Brown
Manganese Brown
Mineral Red
Mummy Brown
Neutral Tint
Payne's Gray
Prussian Brown
Raw Umber (see umber)
Rubens Brown (see Vandyke b.)
Rubens Madder
Sepia
Umber
Vandyke brown

CHAPTER VII.

CHEMICAL REACTIONS OCCURRING BETWEEN TWO OR MORE PIGMENTS, BETWEEN PIGMENT AND VEHICLE, &c.

THE question of the chemical reactions that take place between pigments is one that practically embraces the chemistry of painting. The scope of the present work precludes the possibility of going deeply into this interesting subject, yet it will be of incalculable use both to artist and student to point out some few of the chemical changes that occur between the materials he uses when painting a picture.

Action of Lead and Sulphur.—The reactions that occur between pigments possessing a lead base and pigments possessing sulphur as a component are some of the most destructive, and disastrous to the future permanency of the painting. Briefly the action is this: lead possesses a great affinity for sulphur, consequently these two elements forsake the other components of their respective pigments, unite, and form a new compound—sulphide of lead—which is of a black hue. To take an example: a yellow chromate of lead (*i.e.* ordinary chrome yellow) is mixed with cadmium yellow (*i.e.* the sulphide of cadmium). Watch the result. The lead forsakes the chromate of lead, the sulphur forsakes the cadmium sulphide, and they unite together and form the black sulphide of lead. This action is graphically depicted below.

	Chemical formula of chromate of lead.		Chem. form. of cadmium sulphide.	
Chromium	Cr } set free.		set free Cd	
Oxygen	O_4 }			
Lead . .	Pb .	unites with .	S	=PbS., *i.e.* lead sulphide.

Now both pigments were yellow previous to the formation of this black sulphide of lead, but since a black and yellow produce a green, this will be the resulting hue of the mixture of these two pigments, the greenish tinge becoming stronger and of a deeper green in proportion to the amount of lead converted into sulphide.

Although the chemical change brought about by the union of a lead pigment and one containing sulphur is always the same (*i.e.* the production of lead sulphide), the visual physical change varies. Thus, with the above case of two yellow pigments, we have a visual change into a green hue; this is so, because side by side with the particles of chrome yellow and cadmium yellow there are also particles of black sulphide of lead, and the physical incorporation (for it is not a chemical one, like the union of the lead with the sulphur) of yellow and black particles is the production of a green.

Now it is easily conceivable that a red sulphide, as that of mercury (*i.e.* vermilion) may be mixed with a chrome yellow of lead, whence, after the production of the yellow sulphide, we shall not get a greenish hue, but something different. Thus:

Yellow chrome and red vermilion will produce an orange hue, but as soon as the sulphur in the vermilion unites with the lead in the chrome yellow, we get the black particles of lead sulphide produced, and these commingling with the yellow and red particles of the above pigments change the orange hue into an auburn or brown hue, or to a brownish red, in proportion to the amount of black particles proportionately to the yellow and red ones.

Take another case of this visual physical change. Say a lead chrome is mixed with artificially made ultramarine, and that there is some free sulphur in the ultramarine (*i.e.* that this pigment has been carelessly made, and consequently not entirely freed from this sulphur). The mixture of the yellow chrome and blue ultramarine will produce a green, but in time, as the free sulphur unites with the lead in the chrome, black sulphide of lead appears; and we then get yellow, blue, and black particles heterogeneously mixed, with the result that the visual impression produced by these three colours will no longer be the bright green formed by the blue and yellow, but will be a dark green, approaching black.*

Action of Oxygen amongst Pigments.—Oxygen is an element of much importance as a component of pigments. Its addition to many mineral colours heighten or darken their tone, while its addition to several vegetable colours lessen their tone, or *bleach* them. Likewise the abstraction of oxygen (*i.e.* deoxidation of a pigment) from a mineral pigment weakens its tone.

Let us take some examples. Take chrome yellow of lead again. So long as this yellow remains intact (*i.e.* not decomposed by the influence of other pigments), there is little risk

* The precise hue can be seen by mixing yellow and blue powders, and then adding black powder in various quantities.

of the oxygen in the chrome yellow acting on a pigment affected by oxygen; but suppose, as in the first example, a mixture of lead, chrome, and cadmium yellow is made, the reaction already specified takes place, and consequently the oxygen in the chrome yellow is set free to unite with any other body. This oxygen does enter into union with other bodies, chiefly with the oil used as a vehicle to help dry or harden the oil, and also physically acts on other pigments that are brought within its influence; *e.g.* suppose the mixture of chrome yellow and yellow cadmium glazed with yellow lake, the last pigment will lose its colour, because the oxygen from the chrome will bleach the colour in the yellow lake. If, instead of yellow lake, cochineal lake be glazed over the yellow mixture of lead and cadmium, this crimson colour will in time flee, leaving simply the hue of the yellow beneath.

Again, the abstraction of oxygen from a mineral pigment lessens its tone, while its addition to an animal pigment deepens it; *e.g.* mix an ochre (which has iron as a base) with Naples yellow (which contains oxygen), the iron in the ochre will abstract oxygen from the Naples yellow, and become deeper in tone, due to the oxidation of the iron; whilst its abstraction from the Naples yellow will leave that pigment much weakened in colour, the visual result being a hue totally different to that when the ochre and Naples yellow were first compounded.

There are several other ways in which oxygen plays an important part in the disintegration of paintings, notably in the abstraction of the oxygen from pigments by the oil in drying. Such depletion of oxygen from a pigment leaves that colour an easy prey to injurious influences that would not otherwise act on it, for the simple reason that a partially decayed object is never so sound as a wholly healthy one.

Action of Alkalies on Pigments.—Some pigments are obtained artificially which possess such alkalies as pearlash and soda in their composition; now some few pigments, notably Prussian and Antwerp blues, have their colour destroyed by the action on them of alkalies, consequently they should not be brought into connection with those pigments that have an alkaline base, or which are likely, from their method of manufacture, to possess any free alkali.

The blues above mentioned are turned a buff or tawny drab by the action of alkalies, while yet, again, their colour is restored by any weak acid. Such being the delicacy of Prussian and Antwerp blues, the painter must be very careful in regard to what other pigments he incorporates with them or glazes over them. To know what pigments to avoid in this respect, the painter should consult the chemical nature and composition of the pigments stated in the chapters on pigments given in the first part of this work.

The alkali ammonia is likely to be present in very few pigments, but it is often present in the artist's painting-room or its vicinity. I know one painter whose studio is next door to a stable—in fact, his door opens at right angles to the stable door; consequently it is impossible for him to keep out such ammoniacal fumes as arise from the decaying stable refuse. The action of the fumes of ammonia is not at once apparent, but it is, nevertheless, silently at work, for the fumes insidiously act on the varnish laid on the paintings, disintegrating the varnish; ammonia likewise acts on oils.

There are many other outside influences at work—enemies to the painter and his picture—but in these pages we cannot well discuss them, so I must refer my readers to other works of mine for such information, as it is more properly treated of in those articles from my pen which take up the subject of artists' vehicles. There is one subject, however, that is intimately connected with the pigment and vehicle, and that is *loss of opacity*. This is a term applied to pigments opaque in themselves, but which in time lose their opaqueness, and become so transparent as to allow any colour laid beneath them to become visible. This loss of opacity is notably a characteristic of pigments having lead as a base. The action is a very interesting one.

We have already spoken about the giving up of oxygen from white lead to linseed oil, thus parting with one of its constituents. Oxygen leaves the white lead in a very unstable condition, so much so that the lead particles themselves are at liberty to unite with the linseed oil (other fixed oils have not this effect), and they naturally do so, forming the compound known as linoleate of lead. Now this linoleate of lead (a lead soap, as it is usually called) is easily washed away by sulphuric acid. "But how," my readers will exclaim, "can sulphuric acid get near the painting?" A very natural question, and one easily answered. In this way: sulphur in some form or other is present in vitiated atmospheres, especially so where there is a fire or gas. These sulphurous fumes settle as an opaque film of sooty dust on the painting, and afterwards, from alterations of temperature, moisture settles on the picture also. Now the particles of moisture unite with the sulphurous grime, and form sulphuric acid. The artist, eager to let his picture be seen in all its brilliancy, seizes his silk handkerchief, breathes on the picture, and rubs off the dirt. At the very same operation he is rubbing off some of the lead pigment, because the film of sulphuric acid under his handkerchief unites with the linoleate of lead (that has been produced wherever a lead pigment and linseed oil have been employed) and carries off a thin pellicle of the compound each time he rubs. The amount taken off each time is very minute, but it is none the less surely carried away. We all know how the lacquer on the brass handle of a door will in time wear away by the mere grasping of it in turning the handle. If this hard lacquer can do so, we must readily grant that the more delicate, tender pigment will do so under the rubbing of the handkerchief. The artist, unknowingly, takes a delight in rubbing out his picture, for the more obdurate and obstinate the grime is, the harder and brisker he rubs. The moral to this is, not to use lead pigments in a painting; they are, in fact, the *bête-noire* of the painter. If he, however, *will* continue their employment after this warning, let him at least use an oil (walnut or poppy) that will not form this inimical linoleate of lead.

On the many other changes effected on paintings by the action of oils and other vehicles, the reader is finally referred to articles by the author which have appeared in the pages of the *Artist; Art Journal; Magazine of Art; Art Amateur* (New York); *Painters' Magazine* (New York); *Painting and Decorating* (Philadelphia); *Plumber and Decorator; Decoration; Oil and Colourman's Journal; Oils, Colours, and Drysalteries; Bazaar, Exchange, and Mart*, etc., etc.

CHAPTER VIII.

COLOUR NAMES AND DEFINITIONS.

THE names of colours are still as indefinitely and confusedly used as when Dr. Johnson defined *Brown* as being the "name of a colour composed of black and any other colour," "*Puce*, of a dark brown colour," and "*Pink*, a colour used by painters."

It is truly unfortunate that there is no universal scale of colours. In a letter some years ago to the "Society of Arts Journal," I pointed out the great diversity of names by which colours and pigments are known to the dyer, artist, and ordinary house-painter, and while even authorities on the science of colour disagree as to the so-called primaries, we may expect confusion still to reign. Consequently colours can only be spoken of relatively; *e.g.* we have the blue of cobalt and of the indigo-plant, yet how different in tone, yet both are "blues." If we assume carmine to be the type of pure red, vermilion becomes an orange; and if, on the reverse, we consider vermilion as red, carmine changes to crimson, or belongs to the purple class. The same relation will be found in the tints of gamboge with ochre or yellow cadmium. The purest unmixed primitive colours are to be found in flowers. There can, strictly speaking, be only delicate and full tints of the primary and secondary classes, as the less positive hues being caused by the mixture of the positive colours with their "complementary" hues, are tertiaries and quaternaries.

Positive Colours.—We are accustomed to give the names of positive colours to hues varying from the fullest or brightest tints to very subdued shades.

A Primary colour is one that cannot be compounded by mixture of other colours. I cannot here enter into the question of which colours should be considered as true primaries, but from my own knowledge of colour science I remain steadfast to the old original theory of RED, YELLOW, and BLUE being the three primaries.

Secondary colours are those produced by mixture of any *two* primaries. They are ORANGE, GREEN, and PURPLE, orange being produced by mixture of red and yellow (paints or powders, not coloured lights), green of yellow and blue and purple of red and blue.

Tertiary colours are produced by a mixture of a primary and secondary with one of the colours predominating. They are OLIVE, CITRINE, and RUSSET. "Complementary" colours is a term interchangeable with the primaries and secondaries. Thus, it is theoretically supposed (although in my study of the subject I have failed to come across any scientific reason for this fanciful theory) that complete harmony of colouring is obtained *only* when the three primaries are present, in proportions varying with their intensity of colour. Consequently blue is said to be complementary to orange because it completes the triad of primaries (and, *vice versâ*, orange is complementary to blue); red is complementary to green, and yellow to purple.

Tint is a term used for gradations or mixtures of colours with white.

Hues for mixtures of primary colours with a secondary, or for variations of colour independent of strength, light or dark.

Shade is a term used for the mixtures of colours or hues with black. This term is too often improperly used, when tone should be employed; *e.g.*, many persons in speaking of a lighter tone of, say, a red ribbon, will exclaim, "Oh, what a delicate light *shade!*" when there is not a particle of black in the tone of the red ribbon, but it is, in fact, lighter than the primitive colour. "Shade" should never be used unless black is present in the hue or tone. But the word

Tone should replace it, for this term is applied to any hue, whether it be lighter or darker than the colour of the base; *e.g.* take ultramarine blue as the base colour blue, we should then speak of cobalt as of a lighter tone of blue, and Prussian blue as a darker tone of blue, but we could not properly call Prussian blue a darker *shade* of the blue base ultramarine. Tone expresses the predominant ruling colour or hue in a combination.

Grey.—This is another word improperly applied. When spelt with an *e* the word, amongst colour scientists, refers to a mixture made with black and white, or black and any other colour, bearing in mind that if the two colours do not equally balance to produce the normal grey of the mixture, but that the black predominates and obtrudes itself, the mixture at once becomes a *shade;* at the same time it does not lose its title to grey.

Gray is a term used for a mixture of white and blue, or

when blue replaces black in producing the grayish hue; then we say a bluish *gray* and a blackish *grey*.

As a foundation for a colour scale I would beg to suggest that colours should be named after some well-known flowers, taking the deep yellow of the sunflower as the base for the yellow scale, the poppy or red gladiolus for the base of the red scale, the blue cornflower as the base for the blue scale; and ordinary grass as the base of the green scale.

These bases would not suffice for all the yellow, red, blue, and green tones to be referred to as a "light sunflower yellow," or "dark poppy red," &c., for a lemon yellow could not properly be referred to as a "light sunflower yellow"; but for such pale yellows we could take the primrose as the base, and for the orange hues the skin of the Tangerine orange; for scarlet reds the old standard red geranium, and for the crimson red series we have the deep velvety toned "coxcomb" plant; for the base of the light blue series we could refer to so-and-so lighter tone of the cornflower, because white and a blue of the intensity of this flower would produce a series of true blues varying in tint only in proportion to the amount of white mixed with the blue; for the base colour of the dark series of blues we could not take this flower mixed with black, because black and a blue this colour mixed would produce an indigo hue. We should therefore want to seek some primitive base, as, for instance, the deep, intense blue in the old-fashioned pansy; while for the lighter tones of the green scale we could take the colour of the pyrethrum or featherfew plant as a base, and the dark green leaves of the ivy as a base for the dark series of this scale. I have named these plants, as their colours have up to the present remained constant in hue, and are therefore fitly suited as a standard of reference. It must be borne in mind that the above remarks are only offered suggestively; the scope of such a work as this precludes any lengthened discursive treatment of the question. Yet, nevertheless, it is a work that should not be devoid of any reference to the subject, and any suggestion thrown out may, let me hope, be the means of rousing attention to the question.

The following tabular analysis of the primaries, secondaries, tertiaries, and quaternaries will render it clear to students what colours form the components of some of the complex hues.

Primary Positive Colours.

WHITE.

YELLOW.—There are no distinct general terms for the delicate tints, those in use being borrowed from objects containing them; *e.g.* lemon yellow, straw yellow, primrose.

RED.—The delicate tints, pinks, carnations, rosy.

BLUE.

Secondary Positive Colours, composed of two primaries.

ORANGE, composed of yellow and red; comprehending crimson when the red is in excess.

PURPLE, composed of red and blue. Violet lilac when the red and blue are balanced.

GREEN, composed of yellow and blue. Blue purple when the blue is in excess.

Tertiary Hues, composed of the three primaries with one primary predominating.

CITRINE, where yellow predominates; buff in the lighter hues, tawny or dun in the deeper.

RUSSET, where red predominates; maroon, chocolate.

GREY, where blue predominates.

Quaternary Hues, composed of the primaries with two primaries or a secondary colour predominating.

AUBURN, where orange predominates; brown in the deeper hues.

PUCE, where purple predominates; lavender for the lighter hues, where violet predominates, or the red and blue are balanced.

OLIVE, where the green predominates.

Neutral Tints.

Where the three primaries are in proportion to balance or neutralise each other of which the deeper shade is black.

CHAPTER IX.*

TABLE OF MIXTURES OF PIGMENTS TO PRODUCE BLUES, BUFFS, BROWNS, GREENS, GREYS, PURPLES, AND MAROONS.

Table of Mixtures of Pigments to produce Blues.

Cobalt Green, Cyanine Blue.—In series of blues of the turquoise tint, sparkling and tender, both beautiful and useful.

Table of Mixtures to produce Browns, Buffs, and Yellows.

Chocolate Brown.—Add lake or carmine to burnt umber, or take Indian red and black to form a brown; then add yellow to bring about the desired shade.

Olive Brown.—Mix 1 part of Saxony blue with 3 parts of burnt umber. Change proportions for different shades.

Snuff Brown.—Yellow, 4 parts; Vandyke brown, 2 parts.

Ordinary Brown.—Red, 3 parts; black, 2 parts; yellow, 1 part.

Chestnut Brown.—Red, 2 parts; black, 1 part; Chinese yellow, 2 parts.

Light Buff.—Yellow ochre lightened with white.

* The mixtures named in this chapter are artistically good, but not always so chemically; for their chemical values the reader is referred to the chemical nature of the several pigments named in each mixture.

Deep Buff.—Yellow ochre, white, and a little red.

Oak Colour.—White, 8 parts; yellow ochre, 1 part.

Fawn Colour.—White, 8 parts; red, 1 part; yellow, 2 parts; umber, 1 part.

Tan Colour.—Burnt sienna, 5 parts; yellow, 2 parts; raw umber, 1 part.

Stone Colour.—White, 5 parts; yellow, 2 parts; burnt umber, 1 part.

Brick Colour.—Yellow ochre, 2 parts; red, 1 part; white, 1 part.

Portland Stone Colour.—Raw umber, 3 parts; yellow ochre, 3 parts; white, 1 part.

Yellow Lake.—Umber and white, equal parts; add Naples yellow and scarlet lake; glaze with yellow lake.

Jonquil Yellow.—Mix flake white and Chinese yellow, and add vermilion to carmine.

Golden Yellow.—White and yellow, tinted with red and blue.

Canary Yellow.—White and lemon yellow.

Lemon Colour.—Lemon yellow, 5 parts; white, 2 parts.

Straw Yellow.—Yellow, 5 parts; white, 2 parts; red, 1 part.

Citron.—Red, 3 parts; yellow, 2 parts; blue, 1 part.

Clay Drab.—Raw sienna, raw umber, and white lead, equal parts, and then tint with chrome green.

Ordinary Drab.—White, 9 parts; umber, 1 part.

Cream Colour.—White, 5 parts; yellow, 2 parts; red, 1 part.

Orange.—Made with gamboge and burnt sienna. Useful for the autumnal tints, and to mix with the other greens in order to vary their tone and depth, but not to be used in very warm sky tints.

TABLE OF MIXTURES OF PIGMENTS TO PRODUCE GREYS.

Indigo, lampblack, and madder lake,
Indigo and Indian red.
Indigo and light red.
Indigo, lake, and gamboge.
Indigo, lake, and Roman ochre.
Indigo and Venetian red.
Indigo, raw sienna, and lake.
Indigo, sepia, and lake.
Indigo and purple madder.
Indigo, light red, and lampblack.
Indigo, burnt umber, and lake.
Indigo, madder purple, and burnt umber.
Lampblack and madder lake.
Lampblack and burnt madder.
Lampblack and light red.
Lampblack and lake.

Cobalt green, cyanine blue, carmine madder, for silvery greys, through lilacs to the richest purple.

White, 8 parts; black, 2 parts—for medium grey.

White, 8 parts; blue, 1 part; black, 1 part—lead grey.

White, tinted with ivory black, produces French grey.

White, black, and red, in proportion to suit lustre, for a pearl grey.

Dove Grey.—Red, white, blue, and yellow.

Warm grey is made with Venetian red and indigo. Useful for shadows to warm-coloured objects, and for the colour of earth and mould, and for a tint to put round drawings when mounted.

Purple grey is made with lake and lampblack. Very useful in the grey bark of trees and for rocks; makes various browns mixed with burnt umber and a grey when mixed with Prussian blue or indigo, but not equal to the greys made with lake, gamboge, and indigo, for Prussian blue and lampblack is rather heavy.

Neutral Tint.—Made with Venetian red and indigo and a very little lake. It is a very good tint for cloudy skies, and with the addition of a little blue and lake it makes a pearly grey useful for the shadows to clouds in general.

TABLE OF MIXTURES TO PRODUCE GREENS.

Indigo, light red, and gamboge.

Indigo and gamboge, with either burnt sienna, light red, or Vandyke brown.

Indigo and gamboge.

Indigo, madder purple, and brown pink.

Indigo, burnt umber, and Italian pink.

Indigo and gamboge, with either Roman ochre or lampblack, or raw sienna or lake.

Indigo, Vandyke brown, and yellow ochre.

Indigo and raw sienna.

Indigo and Roman ochre.

Indigo, madder brown, and Indian yellow.

The following for SHADOWS of green :—Indigo and burnt

umber, indigo and Venetian red, indigo and light red, indigo and lake, and gamboge, lampblack, and light red.

Transparent oxide of chromium and cadmium yellow, deep, for the deep rich green and russets of autumn.

Transparent oxide of chromium and aureolin, for the more sunny autumn greens.

Permanent yellow and cobalt green, for the tender spring greens.

Permanent scarlet, carmine madder, for flower painting the crimson-scarlet autumn effects, &c., &c.

Cadmium yellow and Prussian blue or black, for the light, when vivid, of foliage in masses.

Naples yellow, with blue or black, for the grey-greens produced by reflection. Use some white in these tints.

Yellow ochre and blue; where the leaves are brown, the ochres and burnt sienna may be used.

Naples yellow and terra verte is a very useful mixture for the cold greens.

Dutch pink and Prussian blue, foreground glazed with yellow lake, for bottle green.

Pea Green.—White, 5 parts; chrome green, 1 part.

Bronze Green.—Chrome green, 5 parts; black, 1 part; umber, 1 part.

Grass Green.—Yellow, 3 parts; Prussian blue, 1 part.

Willow Green.—White, 5 parts; verdigris, 2 parts.

Olive Green.—Yellow, 8 parts; blue, 1 part; black, 1 part.

Dark Warm Green.—Made with burnt sienna, gamboge, and indigo, is useful for the tints of trees and shadows for grasses, &c., and particularly near foreground.

Warm Green.—Made with the above colours, but differently proportioned, is useful for grass and weeds.

Olive Green.—Made with more burnt sienna and gamboge added to the blue, is very useful for shadows to bright and warmish yellow green.

Table of Mixtures to produce Maroons, Purples, and Pinks.

Wine Colour.—Ultramarine, 2 parts; carmine, 3 parts.

Maroon Colour.—Carmine, 3 parts; yellow, 2 parts.

Carnation Red.—Lake, 3 parts; white, 1 part.

Plum Colour.—White, 2 parts; blue, 1 part; red, 1 part.

Claret Colour.—Red and black, or carmine and blue.

Purple.—Red, white, and blue, variously proportioned.

Lilac.—Red, 4 parts; white, 3 parts; blue, 1 part.

Violet.—Similar to lilac, but bluer than lilac and more red than in purple.

Peach Blossom.—White, 8 parts; red, 1 part; blue, 1 part; yellow, 1 part.

Flesh Colour.—White, 8 parts; red, 3 parts; cadmium, or Naples yellow, 3 parts.

Copper Red.—Red, 1 part; yellow, 2 parts; black, 1 part.

Salmon Pink.—White, 5 parts; yellow, 1 part; umber, 1 part; red, 1 part.

Rose Colour.—White, 5 parts; carmine, 2 parts.

CHAPTER X.

ARTISTIC QUALITIES OF PIGMENTS USED IN PORTRAIT, FLOWER, AND MARINE PAINTING IN WATER COLOURS.

THE COLOURS FOR FLESH ARE—

Brown madder, burnt sienna, cobalt blue, Indian red, Indian yellow, pink madder (rose madder), Vandyke brown, Venetian red (or light red) vermilion, zinc white (*i.e.* Chinese white).

THE COLOURS FOR DRAPERIES AND BODY WASHES BESIDES THE ABOVE LIST ARE—

Carmine, gamboge, French ultramarine, indigo, lake, Prussian blue, sepia, smalt, yellow ochre.

Burnt sienna serves for the shadow tints of amber-coloured draperies; it is also used in some flesh tints.

Brown madder used alone may be used to lower red curtains or draperies, and for the darkest touches in flesh.

Carmine should not be used in flesh, but pink madder is used for the carnation tints in flesh, and for pink draperies.

Cobalt is the best blue pigment for producing the silvery

tints on flesh in painting in water-colours; alone it forms the blue tints, and with Indian red the shadow colour for flesh.

French ultramarine is used only in draperies.

Indian red makes an excellent shadow colour for flesh, both alone and mixed with blue.

Sepia is used for the shadows of white linen and white draperies.

Venetian red is a serviceable colour for general purposes; its tints, though bright, are clear and are very permanent. This pigment is valuable as a general tint for flesh.

Vermilions afford a fine tint for the carnations of flesh.

Vandyke brown gives with lake a fine warm transparent tint which is much used as a warm shadow colour.

Yellow ochre is a useful local colour for light hair.

COLOURS CHIEFLY USED IN FLOWER PAINTING IN WATER COLOURS.

The colours of flowers are so numerous, and the number of tints so indefinite, varying in each particular case with the colour of the flower being copied, that it is almost impossible to set forth a list of tints and mixtures for the flower-painter's use. It is therefore only possible to specify the pigments chiefly used. These are—

Carmine, Chinese white, chrome yellow, cobalt, crimson lake, gamboge, Indian yellow, Indian red, indigo, pink madder, sepia, Vandyke brown.

The following colours are seldom used :—

Chrome yellow deep, French blue, lemon yellow, scarlet, smalt.

The following table comprises the list of *opaque* colours used in flower painting :—

Reds.—Vermilion, Indian red.

Yellows.—Chrome of various depths, yellow ochre.

The following list gives the *semi-opaque* pigments :—

Reds.—Venetian red.

Yellows.—Raw sienna.

Blues.—Cobalt blue, French blue, ultramarine.

Browns.—Burnt umber, madder brown.

The following list comprises the *transparent* pigments:—

Reds.—Extract of madder, carmine, pink madder, lake.

Yellows.—Gamboge, Indian yellow.

Blues.—Antwerp blue, indigo.

Browns.—Vandyke brown, burnt sienna, violet, carmine, madder purple (semi-transparent).

In painting Sea Views in Water Colours, many of the Colours already mentioned are very useful; thus—

Cobalt is useful for skies and the remote points of sea and low lands; and a mixture of cobalt, vermilion, madder lake, and yellow ochre may be used for the sky and the clouds in calm weather.

Burnt sienna is an excellent useful colour for the warm tints in rocks, mud, boats, and buildings. For the foresea, whether calm or broken by waves, it is employed with a little madder; and mixed with lampblack and a little madder it makes the tints of old posts, boats, and a variety of near objects; and the tints may be varied by modifying the proportions of the component colours.

Indigo is employed for moonlights, and when mixed with a little lampblack it is well suited for night clouds, distant cliffs, &c. With a little raw umber and madder it may be used for water in night effects. With madder and burnt sienna it is useful for dark rocks and skies, and mixed with raw sienna may also be employed for boats.

Lampblack is a colour which, when mixed with madder and burnt sienna, may be used for dark foreground objects.

Light red is employed with cobalt for the dark tints of the clouds; a thin wash of light red in the lights of the clouds produces mellowness. It is effective as shadow tints, and with indigo makes a good grey.

Madder, with cobalt and a very little yellow ochre, meets the airy tint of the remotest distances, and with burnt sienna and Prussian blue it is well adapted for the shadows of boats, figures, distant hills, and near water.

Madder brown.—Mixed with cobalt this is a valuable shadow colour for distant objects. With indigo it is valuable for shades of objects nearer the foreground. It is a good shade colour when mixed with lampblack, and it is advantageous in rusty iron, as anchors, chains, &c., and in all reds it forms a good shade tint, but for distant red flags it would be advantageous to qualify it with a blue, and for the deepest and reddest part of foreground it may be employed alone, as also for all deep and dark cracks and fissures, or stony markings, in all near objects, as boats, figures, &c.

Sepia is sometimes used alone and sometimes mixed with lampblack or indigo and madder, for dark foregrounds, boats, near rocks, seaweed, &c.

Vermilion is useful for morning and evening skies, whether stormy or tranquil. Vermilion with yellow ochre and cobalt will produce a very pure effect. In the darker grounds of the clouds a little light red may be added. Vermilion, with burnt sienna and madder, is a valuable tint in old houses, piers, &c., and also for shipping and boats in the middle and extreme distances.

Yellow ochre is valuable in warm skies, the sails of ships and boats, sandstone rocks and cliffs, buildings, &c. It does not mix kindly with any of the cold colours, and should therefore be used as a wash over other colours that are dry, when required to qualify their tints.

CHAPTER XI.

ARTISTIC QUALITIES OF COLOURS USED IN LANDSCAPE PAINTING IN OILS.

Colours for Foliage.—For the darker greens, terra verte, black, and Naples yellow, or raw sienna with black and Naples yellow, may be used, as well as the mixtures named in the table of "Green Mixtures."

Colours for Fields.—For the cold greenish grey of unripe oats, use blue, black, and Naples yellow, with, perhaps, a little blue. In ripe oats, use white and Naples yellow, varied by a little yellow ochre. The rich golden hue of ripe wheat will require Naples yellow, with raw and burnt sienna; and for grasses the various greens given in "Green Mixtures" will be found useful.

In Heaths and such-like coloured lands.—Lake with white for the lights, and rich brown for the dark background. For purple heath, French ultramarine, lake, and white. For broom and furze, chrome yellow, reddened with burnt sienna or Naples yellow, as occasion requires, will give the yellow blossom of the broom and furze.

For Birch and Beech.—The silvery greys of the birch or beech may be obtained by black and white, broken, as occasion requires, by a little red or brown. The rich warm browns in the trunks of the birch may be made by burnt sienna and lake, or raw sienna.

Colours for Skies.—These are white, ultramarine, or the permanent blues, blue-black, Indian red, light red, or Mars orange, with light Naples yellow. In deep sunset effects, cadmium yellow and vermilion or carmine may be required.

For Roads.—The various colours of roads may be obtained by mixtures of Indian red, broken with (white in all cases) umber (and lake, as in some of the roads where the old Devonian rocks abound, as in Devonshire); yellow ochre, varied with red, white, or with Naples yellow; burnt sienna, with white broken by umber; grey, broken with red and white; Indian red, black and white, and burnt sienna. Indeed, almost every colour may be mixed with white, so varied are the colour-tones of the earth.

Sir F. Leighton's (P.R.A.) Palette.—Ivory black, cappah brown, burnt sienna, raw sienna, Roman ochre, yellow ochre, jaune de Naples (French Naples yellow), aureolin, cadmium. The following are supplementary: Lemon yellow, pale and dark, flake white, vermilion, Venetian red, Indian red, rose madder, cobalt, emerald, oxide of chromium. *For skies.* Cobalt, pale lemon, vermilion. *For flesh.* Cobalt and emerald, oxides of chromium (mixed with white in gradations), vermilion and lake (mixed with white in gradations), yellow ochre, Roman ochre, burnt sienna.

Alma-Tadema's (R.A.) Palette. — White, Naples yellow, yellow ochre, raw sienna, brown ochre, cadmium (rarely), orange vermilion, Chinese vermilion, light red or burnt yellow ochres, madder lake (seldom used), burnt sienna, cobalt green, oxide of chromium, ivory black.

Armitage's (R.A.) Palette.—White, Naples yellow, yellow ochre, raw sienna, light red, burnt sienna, vermilion, oxide of chromium, cobalt, madder lake, black.

Orchardson's (R.A.) Palette.—White, lemon yellow, yellow ochre, vermilion, Indian red, crimson lake or madder, Vandyke brown, Antwerp blue. The following are supplementary: Cadmium, raw sienna, light red, gold ochre, black.

Pettie's (R.A.) Palette.—White, lemon or yellow, raw sienna, yellow ochre, cadmium, vermilion, crimson madder, cobalt, Vandyke brown, ivory black. The following are supplementary: Purple madder, French ultramarine, Antwerp or Prussian blue, Caledonian brown.

Colin Hunter's Palette.—White, Naples yellow, lemon yellow, yellow ochre, raw sienna, cadmium, pale and deep vermilion, rose madder, cobalt, Antwerp blue, burnt sienna, madder brown, Vandyke brown, Caledonian brown, or cappah brown.

CHAPTER XII.

QUESTIONS SET AT THE SOUTH KENSINGTON SCHOOL OF ART EXAMINATIONS IN PAINTING.

THE following are some few of the questions that are asked in Group 2, subject Painting. The questions are so asked as to compel the student to make himself acquainted with more than a mere superficial knowledge of the old methods of painting. Such being the case, it would be manifestly unfair for me to answer the questions here, and it would be of little service to the student were I to do so, because, although I answered all these, perhaps at the next examination in the subject, totally different questions, although in kindred topics, might be asked; moreover, the answers that would be given in this work would be little better than would suffice for "cram work," which is a system of learning I am strongly against. I have seen students, a few days before the examination, get the papers of questions set at previous examinations, take the questions seriatim, and then vainly endeavour to find answers in some elementary text-book on art. In such a work they get a mere toutline of the various modes of painting, &c., and the subjects are probably so baldly treated that there is nothing tangible he student can digest, so he endeavours to repeat, parrot-like, what he finds set forth; but the outline is so bare that it is a mere skeleton of an answer he can give, a skeleton that can fit into more than one suit of clothes (*i.e.* answer questions in a general way), but yet do duty to none. Such cramming is highly injurious to the students, and is productive of ludicrous answers to the examination questions.

Rather than help towards such a system of cramming, I have determined not to give here the answers to these questions, but prefer to direct the student to the fountain-head. This I do because I have noticed many students know not in the least what authority to consult, and also because I feel sure that by directing them to the right authority, irrespective of the special place in such work, the student will incidentally be induced to dip deeper into the subject by perhaps reading through, if not studying, those works, than he would do were he to find the answers cut and dried ready to hand.

Questions 1, 2, 3, 4, 5 and 6 can be readily answered by consulting the paragraphs on the "Chemical Names and Composition," and the paragraphs on "Permanency" and "Non-Permanency," in the chapters on the various pigments given in the first part of this book.

To answer *question* 7, see "Cennini Cennino's Treatise on Painting" (translated by Mrs. Merrifield, 1844), chapter 67, "The manner of painting on walls, that is, in Fresco, and of colouring the faces of young persons," pages 39—44.

Questions 8, 9, 10, 11, 12 can be answered by studying the information given in Mrs. Merrifield's work on "Fresco Painting" (1846), in the pages 18 to 23:—"How to lay on the coats of plaster, the various kinds of *intonochi*, and the preparation of the mortars."

See also "Of painting on walls, and why it is called Fresco," pages 30, 31, same book.

See also "Of preparing the walls," pages 45—51, *ibid.*

See also "Inquiry whether the ancients painted in Fresco," page 62, *ibid.*

See also "The execution of frescoes," page 63, and of the colours, cartoons, and painting, page 65, *ibid.*

Likewise see "The practice of fresco painting" (according to the directions and observations of Palomino) at page 70 of above book, and also "Of preparing the stucco," page 71; "Preparation of the walls," page 72; "Of laying on the intonaco," page 72; "On using the cartoons," pages 73—76; "Of the colours used," pages 76—81. See also page xi. of Introduction, "Colours used in fresco."

Reference to the above sections of this work and to the following in Cennini's treatise, "How to colour walls in secco, and what tempera is proper for that purpose," pages 47—49, chap. 72; and also "How to colour pictures and to temper the colours," page 87, chap. 145, same work; together with a perusal of the section on "Fresco" in Mr. Cave Thomas's work on "Mural Decoration," and the article "Fresco," in the "English Encyclopædia," vol. xiv., page 240 (1860 ed.), will give the student so much information on fresco, and so well ground him in the practice of the old masters, that he will be able to answer any question set relative to this style of painting.

To answer *questions* 13 and 14, refer to Cennini's treatise, pages 9, 16, 32, 128, and xiv. of Introduction; "Biacca (white lead): its nature, properties, and use;" "Bianco San-Giovanni: its nature, properties, and use," see pages 31, 127, 128, *ibid.*

See also pages 41, 53, of "Verdaccio, a compound colour," in above work.

To answer *question* 15, refer to Cennini, pages 43, 44, "To paint the head of a young person as taught by Giotto."

Questions 16 and 17 may be answered by reading up "Painting in distemper: its advantages and disadvantages," pages xvi. and 156 of Cennini.

See also, page 87, "How to temper the colour for distemper," and "How to paint in distemper," page 87. "Directions for softening the tint," page 156, and "Where distemper cannot be employed," page 56; and "Distemper invented by Ludius, in the time of Augustus," page 144. See also pages 47, 87, 96 of Cennini; and see also Mrs. Merrifield's book on "Fresco Painting," pages 77, 78.

Question 18 may be answered by reading through "Hogarth's Analysis of Beauty."

All, or almost all, the other questions usually set at this examination may be answered by consulting Eastlake's "Materials for a History of Oil Painting."

Question 1.—Describe the relative durability of the following colours and their chemical ingredients respectively: zinc white, flake white, cadmium yellow, vermilion, colcothar, cobalt blue, cappah brown, Cologne earth, masticot, chrome yellow.

Question 2.—Lemon yellow, orpiment, yellow ochre,

Roman ochre, chrome yellow, cadmium. State which of these colours is considered durable.

Question 3.—Describe the chemical properties and the comparative durability or otherwise of the following colours: terra verde, chrome green, malachite green, verdigris, Naples yellow, orpiment.

Question 4.—Describe the chemical constituents and the comparative durability or otherwise of vermilion, light red, Indian red, cadmium, lemon yellow, cobalt, indigo, verdigris, scarlet lake.

Question 5.—Mention the principal colours derived from the following substances, and their comparative durability: 1, copper; 2, arsenic; 3, mercury; 4, sodium; 5, lead.

Question 6.—What were the grounds for oil painting used by the early Flemings? Were they absorbent, and of what colour?

Question 7.—Describe the difference between "fresco secco" and "fresco buono," and detail the principal processes employed in each.

Question 8.—What colours are chiefly employed in fresco buono? Describe in detail the processes of painting during the day. What is the effect of mixing terra verde with lime?

Question 9.—How is the cartoon prepared for fresco painting and transferred to the "intonaco"? In what state should the latter be (as to moisture) on commencing each day's work?

Question 10.—Describe the various ingredients and the proportions of each for preparing the "intonaco" in fresco painting. Is there any time during which lime may be kept for the purpose of fresco painting? If so, state the reasons for the limitation.

Question 11.—For what reason is it necessary to keep lime before using it in fresco painting? Describe the preparation of the walls and the work to be done by the plasterer before commencing the operation which causes the colour to adhere to its surface, and what prevents its adhesion.

Question 12.—Why was terra verde so much used by fresco painters, and what effect has it on lime whites?

Question 13.—What are the pigments called by Cennini biacco and bianco di San-Giovanni?

Question 14.—What is biacca, bianco, San-Giovanni, verdacio as described by Cennini?

Question 15.—How did Giotto paint a head in fresco as described by Cennini?

Question 16.—How were the walls (1), panels (2), prepared for painting on in distemper during the sixteenth century?

Question 17.—What is the process of tempera painting: (1) the panel and its preparation, (2) the vehicle, (3) the procedure? Was oil varnish ever employed in connection with tempera painting?

Question 18.—What qualities does Hogarth say are essential to beauty?

Question 19.—Who were the earliest artists to practise oil painting in Italy? From whom did they derive the knowledge, and when and where did they flourish?

Question 20.—What method did the first colourists adopt

to secure richness of effect in pictures when seen at a considerable distance, as in churches?

Question 21.—Describe Van Eyck's supposed method of painting, from the design to the completion of a picture, and his vehicle. What portion of a picture did he usually commence to paint in colour?

Question 22.—Did Rubens avail himself of much preparatory labours in commencing his pictures? Describe his usual mode of practice.

Question 23.—In what particulars did the Venetian method differ from that of Rubens?

Question 24.—What opinion did Rubens hold about the necessity of studying the antique marbles and bronzes?

Question 25.—What was the method of painting said to have been adopted by the ancient Greeks, and with what vehicles, and were the pictures so executed durable?

Question 26.—Who principally originated the Florentine method of painting, and in what respects did it vary from the method taught by the Flemings?

Question 27.—In what method are the works of Giotto and his school usually executed?

Question 28.—What were the relations existing between L. da Vinci and Michael Angelo? Was there any instance of pictorial rivalry?

Question 29.—Who were the principal painters of the later Flemish school (seventeenth century)? Describe the usual methods of painting, (1) as to the material or ground, (2) as to practice.

Question 30.—What vehicle is said to have been adopted by Van Dyke in oil painting?

Question 31.—State which of the schools of art (in the sixteenth century) made many drawings for their pictures, and who. Give examples of varieties of process, and trace their different results.

Question 32.—State the methods of preparing grounds for oil painting employed by the early Flemish and Italian painters, the various modifications in later practice, and the comparative advantages and disadvantages of each.

Question 33.—What causes cracks in painting? What causes a wrinkled surface?

Question 34.—Describe the various "media" or vehicles used in pictures by (1) the ancient Greeks, (2) the tempera painters during the fourteenth and fifteenth centuries, (3) in the transition period, (4) by the Van Eycks.

Question 35.—Did Cennini know the uses of varnish?

Question 36.—Were resinous vehicles ever varied according to the colours in the same picture, or was it usual to adopt one uniform vehicle throughout, during the sixteenth century?

Question 37.—What proportions did the various resins bear to the oil in making varnishes for painting?

Question 38.—What is the method supposed to have been adopted by the great Venetian painters in commencing their pictures, and in what respect was it different from the Florentine and Roman schools?

Question 39.—What were the grounds for oil painting used by the early Flemings? Were they absorbent, and of what colour?

Question 40.—To what school did Sebastian del Piombo belong? Who were his masters?

Question 41.—What evidence can you give of the practice of modelling figures, in wax or clay, by any of the great colourists before commencing their pictures?

Question 42.—Describe the gradual change of method from tempera to oil painting, the vehicles employed, and their composition. Was more than one vehicle employed in the same picture?

Question 43.—What were the methods of oil painting in the Venetian School in Bellini's time, what changes did they undergo, and to whom were the changes attributed?

Question 44.—Who was the master of Giovanni Bellini?

Question 45.—Who was Michael Angelo's first master in painting? Relate some of the circumstances connected with his first attempts in sculpture.

Question 46.—Trace slightly the course of art from its revival in the thirteenth century; the various schools, and the names of the founders or principal painters in each school, down to the end of the sixteenth century.

[Note.—The questions given above are those which were set to Art Students ten years ago. As, however, they cover the whole ground of the Art Student's curriculum, they have not lost their value at the present time.—H. C. S., *July*, 1896.]

INDEX.

THE END.

PRINTED BY J. S. VIRTUE AND CO., LIMITED, CITY ROAD LONDON.

K/S

www.ingramcontent.com/pod-product-compliance
Ingram Content Group UK Ltd.
Pitfield, Milton Keynes, MK11 3LW, UK
UKHW020714111225
9512UKWH00047B/1089

9 781013 772924